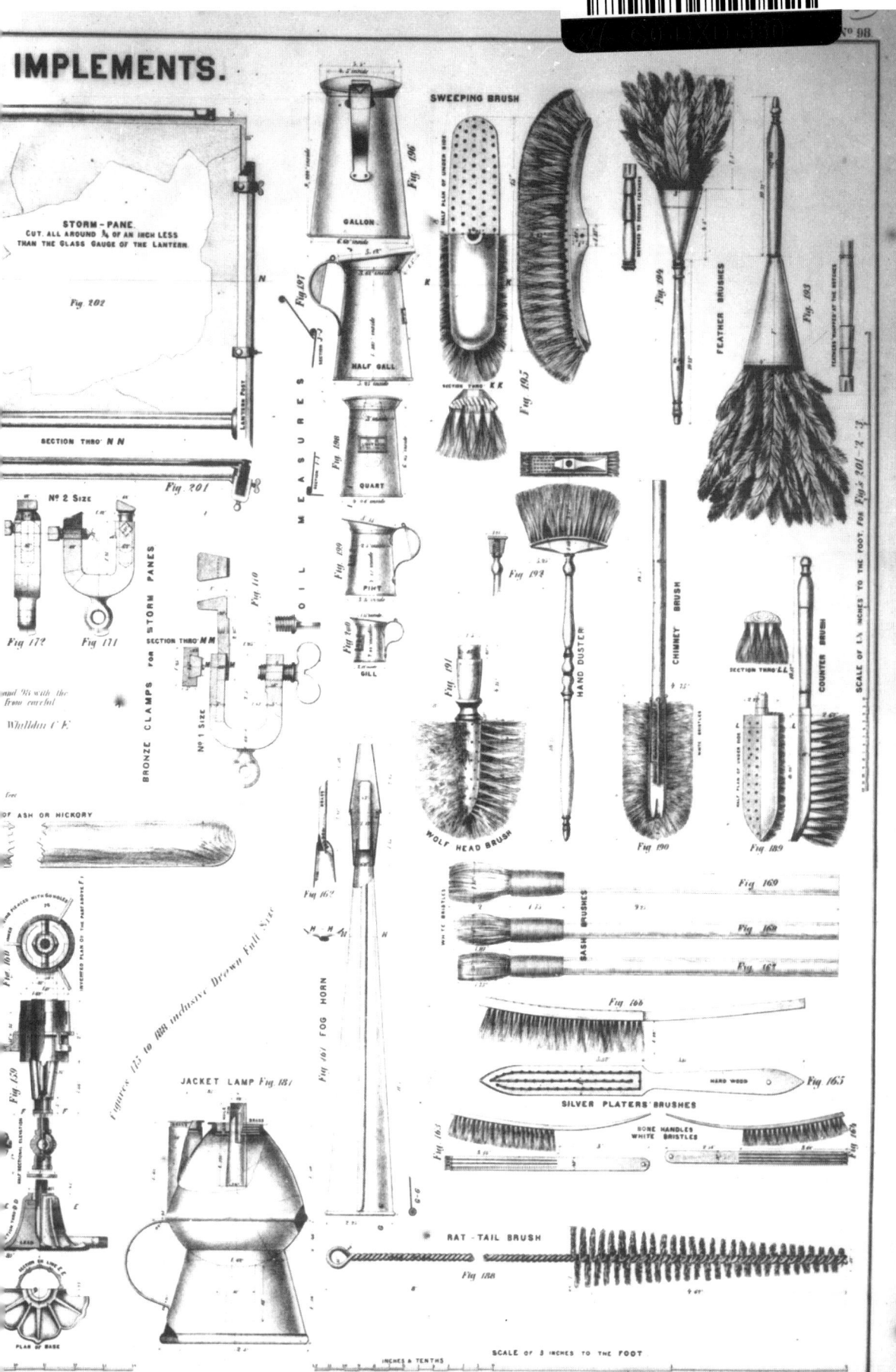

Previous pages:
The nineteenth-century lighthouse keeper had an array of tools from clamps for holding broken lantern panes to glazier's pincers to feather dusters for cleaning the lens. Some are shown in these drawings published by the U.S. Lighthouse Establishment.

Beacons of Hooper Strait

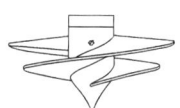

Norman H. Plummer

Published by
Chesapeake Bay Maritime Museum
St. Michaels, Maryland

Chesapeake Bay Maritime Museum
St. Michaels, Maryland 21663
© 2000 by Chesapeake Bay Maritime Museum
All rights reserved
Printed in the United States of America

      Library of Congress Cataloging-in-Publication Data

Plummer, Norman H.
   Beacons of Hooper Strait / Norman H. Plummer.
     p. cm.
   Includes bibliographical references and index.
   ISBN 0-922249-08-3
     1. Hooper Strait Light Station (Md.) I. Title

VK1025.H66 P58 2000
387.1'55'0975227--dc21

                                                    00-030331

Library of Congress Control Number 00-131774

Nothing indicates the liberality, prosperity, or intelligence of a nation more clearly than the facilities which it affords for the safe approach of the mariner to its shores.

Light-House Board Report, 1868

Contents

Preface .... *v*
Introduction .... *vii*
I. Hooper Strait Lightships 1
II. Hooper Strait Lighthouses 17

Appendices
1. Keepers of Lightships and Lighthouses 55
2. Screwpile Lighthouses of Chesapeake Bay 58
3. Transcript of Contract for Construction of
   First Hooper Strait Lightship 60
4. Transcript of Contract for Construction of
   Second Hooper Strait Lightship (1845) 66
5. Description of the Foundations for the Second
   Hooper Strait Lighthouse 70
6. Engineer's Estimates of Cost of Second
   Hooper Strait Lighthouse 71
7. Description of Property Ceded to the United States by
   Governor of Maryland for Second Hooper Strait Lighthouse . 72

Notes
Abbreviations Used in Notes 75
I. Hooper Strait Lightships 76
II. Hooper Strait Lighthouses 80

    Bibliography 85
    Index 87
    Picture Credits 93

Preface

The Hooper Strait light station has endured since 1827. The lighthouse structure, now owned by the Chesapeake Bay Maritime Museum, was not built until 1879, but the fifty-two years of history that preceded it as well as the story of the existing building deserve to be compiled. That is what we have tried to accomplish in this monograph by looking at myriad letters, documents, drawings, and other material safely salted away in the United States National Archives. Probably we have failed to find every treasure from Hooper Strait in that tremendous storehouse, but we share here what we did find.

A note on spelling: We used the term "Hooper Strait" when it does not appear in quotations because that designation appears on present-day charts; however, to keep quotations from early documents intact, we used "Hooper's," "Streights," and "Straights."

My thanks to all who contributed to this effort, especially John and Angie Vander Eedt at the archives, whom we drove to distraction with our requests and who were immensely helpful in leading us to the letters of keepers, superintendents, auditors, and engineers; Shawn Aubitz at the archives' Philadelphia branch, who found architectural drawings of both the present lighthouse and its predecessor; Ann House at the Steamship Historical Society of America, who kindly assisted in locating photographs of lighthouse cutters and tenders; the museum's curator, Pete Lesher, who was invaluable in making technical suggestions; and Marty King, who deserves high praise for editing and laying out the manuscript with sensitivity, understanding, and efficiency.

Above all, Ellen Plummer persevered through thick—sometimes very thick—and thin in searching for the prints and photographs, proofreading, and keeping the author on track.

Norman H. Plummer

Introduction

Maritime transportation has been a critical factor in Maryland's economic growth, particularly prior to the development of railway lines, road systems, and airports. Lighthouses, more correctly termed light stations, as well as navigational buoys and fog signals played a significant role in the economic growth and development of Maryland by helping to create a crucial and safe maritime transportation network. Light stations are the principal and most historically significant element of this extensive system of aids to navigation that developed on the Chesapeake Bay and its tributaries. Hooper Strait Light Station represents one of forty-nine light stations established in the Maryland portion of the bay and its tributaries between 1821 and 1910.

In the early years of Maryland's development there was no systematic establishment of aids to navigation such as buoys or lighthouses to assure safe passage of vessels into and through the Chesapeake Bay and its tributaries. It is estimated that thirty to forty ships were employed in the tobacco trade in the Chesapeake in 1633 which had increased to about 300 vessels by 1776. Yet, prior to the 1770s no publicly funded aids to navigation were known, and from the 1770s until Cape Henry lighthouse was first lit in 1792, there were only six buoys in the entire Chesapeake Bay, and those marked shoals at the entrance to the bay. Individuals, plantations, and some ports no doubt used simple poles and branches to mark shoals and other hazards to navigation, but these were not regulated and were largely understood only by locals. The first aids to navigation provided by the federal government in Maryland waters are believed to have been buoys authorized by Congress in an act dated 3 March 1819 for marking the Patapsco River.

Of the twenty-four lighthouses in the United States in 1800, none had yet been built in Maryland. Noted Chesapeake colonial historian

Arthur Pierce Middleton stated, "Chesapeake Bay, with a greater volume of shipping than any other region of the continental America in the eighteenth century, was the last important region to be provided with the benefits of so useful an aid to navigation [as a lighthouse]."

By 1820 there were fifty-five lighthouses on the East Coast of the United States of which four were built in the Virginia portion of the Chesapeake Bay; but still not one had been built in Maryland. The following year two lightships began operation in Maryland waters, one at Upper Cedar Point on the Potomac River, 1821-1867, and another off the mouth of the Potomac at Smith Point, 1821-1868.

By 1910 the United States Lighthouse Bureau reported 1,397 light stations, 3,992 lighted aids, and 6,507 unlighted aids, 457 of which were fog signals. This was the golden age of lighthouses for Maryland with forty-two active light stations. Never were there more operational light stations in Maryland than between the turn of the century and the first decade of the twentieth century.

Of the forty-nine light stations established in Maryland waters between 1821 and 1910, only twenty-six retain extant structures. Many of these light station sites had more than one structure built upon them over time due to erosion, fire, destructive ice floes, and changing technology. Hooper Strait Light Station, for example, had two lightships and two screwpile lighthouses sequentially occupying its site between 1827 and the present. In 1966 the wooden keepers' cottage and tower portion of the structure were moved to the grounds of the Chesapeake Bay Maritime Museum; but the cast iron screwpile foundation remains intact upon which a modern aid to navigation sits. All told there were over one hundred light station structures, including lightships, built or moored in Maryland waters. The surviving light stations, sixteen of which are still functioning as active aids to navigation, are significant links to this past. The preservation and interpretation of Hooper Strait Light Station by the Chesapeake Bay Maritime Museum helps citizens and visitors alike better appreciate and understand this important and interesting aspect of our maritime heritage.

Perhaps as many as one hundred screwpile-type lighthouses with cottage-like keepers' quarters were built throughout the Carolina sounds, the Chesapeake Bay, Delaware Bay, and along the Gulf of Mexico; one was even built at Maumee Bay, Lake Erie, Ohio. However, the Chesapeake, with forty-two, has the distinction of having had the most screwpile lighthouse structures of any equal-sized area in the world. Of these forty-two Chesapeake screwpile lighthouses, nineteen were built in Maryland waters. Only four screwpile lighthouses survive in Maryland, and three of the four have been transplanted to onshore settings: Sevenfoot Knoll relocated to the Inner Harbor of Baltimore, Drum Point relocated to the Calvert Marine Museum, and Hooper Strait relocated to the Chesapeake Bay Maritime Museum. Only Thomas Point Shoals screwpile light station retains its cottagelike keepers' quarters and remains at its original location. The Chesapeake Bay Maritime Museum was the first museum in the Chesapeake tidewater area, and possibly in the world, to move, restore and interpret for the public a relocated lighthouse structure. While the staff of the museum may not have realized it at the time, they could not have picked a more appropriate lighthouse construction type, as the screwpile lighthouse has become an icon for the Chesapeake Bay region.

Norman Plummer's *Beacons of Hooper Strait* is the most comprehensive history of man's attempt to navigationally mark this important passage between Hooper Island and Bishops Head on the north and Bloodsworth Island on the south. Ships plying Tangier Sound from the Wicomico and Nanticoke rivers and Crisfield, Maryland, an important seafood harvesting and processing region of the bay, to points north use this strait as it is the most direct route. The strait's importance is demonstrated by it being marked by one of the earliest lightships to serve in Maryland's waters, operating from 1827 to 1867 (two lightships began operation in 1821 to mark the Potomac River).

The Chesapeake Bay Maritime Museum is to be commended for its efforts to preserve the Hooper Strait lighthouse and for undertaking this comprehensive research of its history. In a sense, the story of the political struggle to obtain funds for the construction of the Hooper Strait light station, the story of those keepers that dealt with the tedium of operating such an isolated light station, the stories of interesting and sometimes frightful incidents such as a ship sinking or the lighthouse being plucked up by ice and moved over four miles off station, and stories of surviving storms are, in general, the story of many Chesapeake Bay lighthouses, only each slightly different. Therefore, this lighthouse history gives the reader not only a thorough understanding of the history of the Hooper Strait lighthouse but also a general understanding of Chesapeake lighthouse history. Readers of this history are encouraged to explore the lighthouses of the Chesapeake, especially those interpreted and open to the public. They are well worth a visit.

Ralph E. Eshelman
Lusby, Maryland
23 March 2000

I.
Hooper Strait Lightships

Visitors to the Chesapeake Bay Maritime Museum are familiar with the Hooper Strait Lighthouse which dominates Navy Point and the museum's logo. The lighthouse marked the Hooper Strait shoals until it was moved in 1966, but long before it was built, two lightboats successively served as aids to navigation at the same station. They were built in response to local demand, manned by local men, and for many years helped local mariners make their way through the twisting channel between the Chesapeake Bay and Tangier Sound. Lightships were a relatively simple way to provide navigational aids at shifting shoals near the mouths of rivers and straits where construction of lighthouses was difficult.

In 1787 Congress created the United States Light House Establishment as part of the Treasury Department. The few lighthouses then existing were taken over by the federal government. In 1820, the Treasury assigned responsibility for all lighthouses, lightships, and buoys to its Fifth Auditor and Acting Commissioner of Revenue, Stephen Pleasonton. The tight-fisted Pleasonton was conservative about improving navigation aids and caused the United States to lag behind the Europeans in adopting the most advanced methods. He held that position until 1852 when, after an investigation into irregularities in his department, he was replaced by the Light-House Board composed of two senior naval officers, an officer of the army engineers, two civilians of "high scientific attainment," and one lower-grade naval officer who served as secretary. Pleasonton and then the Light-House Board were ultimately responsible for the Hooper Strait Light Station. The Board remained under the Treasury Department until 1903, when it was renamed the Light House Service and moved to the newly created Department of Commerce where it was renamed the Bureau of Lighthouses in 1910. The bureau remained in the Commerce Department until 1939 when it was consolidated with the Coast Guard and then moved to the Department of Transportation in 1968.[1]

During the 1820s, the "Era of Internal Improvement," Congress was pressured by states and individuals to finance roads and canals throughout the East, and maritime communities also sought help. Congress acted: The annual report of the lighthouse service for 1841 showed that between 1817 and 1830 the number of lighthouses in the United States increased from 52 to 142, and the number of lightships from none in 1819 to sixteen in 1830.

When Joseph Kent (1779-1837) became governor of Maryland in January 1826, he made it his mission to encourage improvement of the natural resources enjoyed by the state. As a member of the United States Congress, he had taken part in the debates on public works. Now he promoted Maryland's role in the Chesapeake & Ohio Canal, urged the state to support the Baltimore & Ohio Railroad, and put before the General Assembly numerous road and bridge-building projects. The advantages of these projects to the western shore of the Chesapeake Bay were evident, but Eastern Shore residents wanted a share of the pie. Maryland Assembly delegate Littleton Dennis Teackle (1777-1848) of Princess Anne became their spokesman. He believed navigational improvements were linked to general transportation improvement, and better navigation in the Chesapeake and its tributaries would facilitate the use of the state's natural resources. Teackle drew up petitions calling on the "parental regard" of Congress to establish lightships and lighthouses on the lower shore. The petitions pointed out that "a large portion of property to a vast amount, & many valuable lives wrecked and lost by storms and tempests would have been avoided and saved by the…establishment of a Beacon or Light Boat on Hooper's island bar in Hooper's Streights" [2] and other locations. They were signed by 121

Hooper Strait is the most direct route for vessels sailing from Baltimore to Deal Island and the Hongu, Nanticoke, and Wicomico Rivers on the Eastern Shore. The lightboats and first lighthouse marked the shoal on the south side of the strait; the second lighthouse was built on the north side. ▶

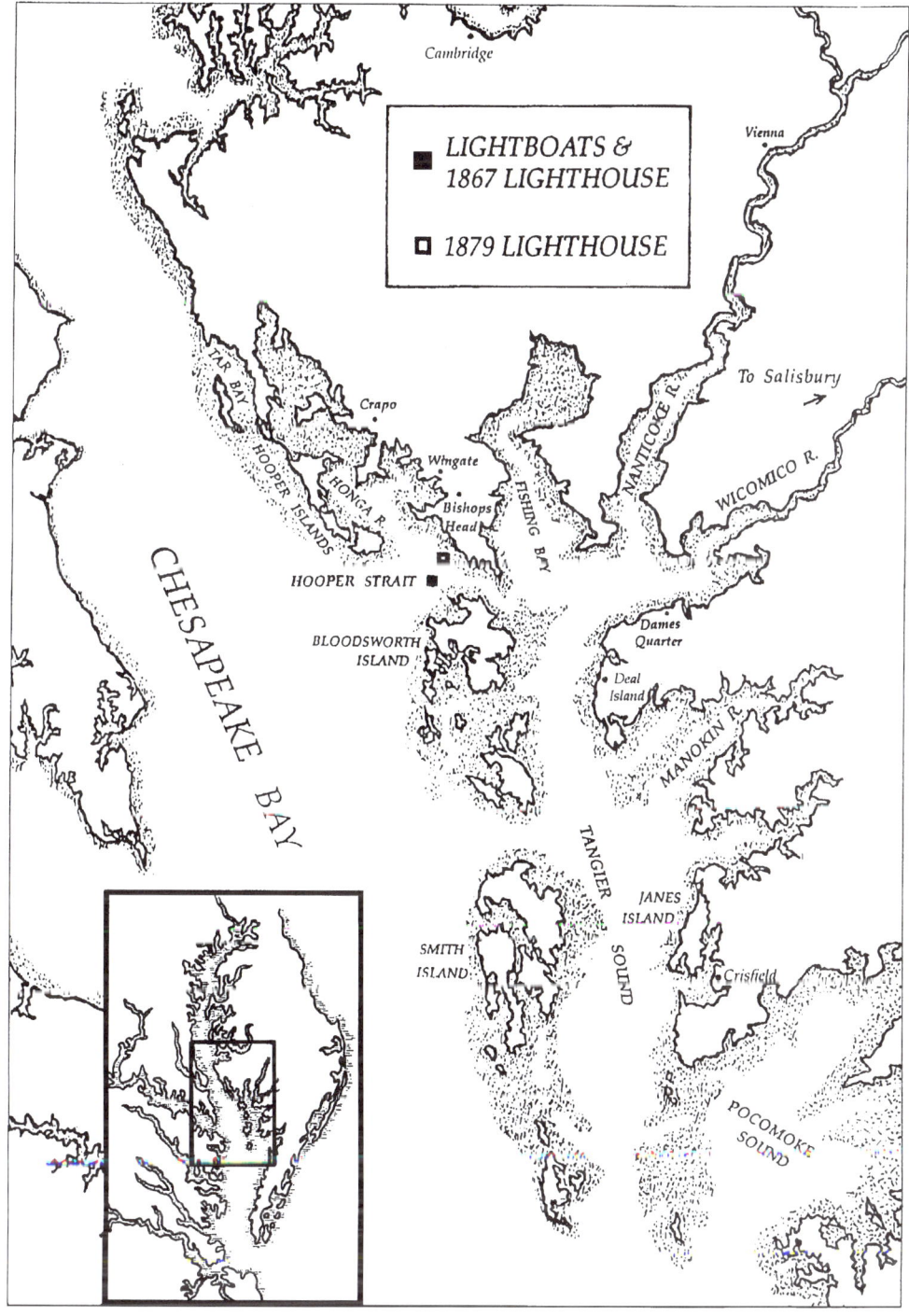

"inhabitants of...Maryland & Virginia in behalf of ourselves and others concerned in the Trade and Navigation of the Chesapeake and its several sounds, bays, rivers, and Creeks...."[3]

First Lightship
Legislators did not provide for light stations without prodding. In February 1826, the Maryland General Assembly passed, and Governor Kent sent to Maryland's senators and representatives, a resolution drafted by delegate Teackle calling on each to use his influence to procure the erection of lighthouses on Fogs Point and Smith Island and a "Light Boat in Hoopers Streights."[4]

Why did Hooper Strait need a navigational aid? The answer can be found in a chart of the area which shows that Hooper Strait provides the most direct access for ships traveling between the northern parts of the bay and towns on the rivers flowing into Tangier Sound. Delegate Teackle, who might well be called the "father of the Hooper Strait light boat," noted that "although meandering, it [Hooper Strait] is wide and practicable for Vessels of 12 feet [draft]...." By 1826, Vienna on the Nanticoke River at the north end of Tangier Sound and Snow Hill on the Pocomoke were already ports of entry with considerable shipping.[5]

On receipt of the petitions and resolutions, Thomas Newton (1768-1847), congressman from Norfolk, Virginia, and chairman of the House Commerce Committee, asked for further information. One reply came from Captain John Ferguson who observed that a light vessel in "Hooper's Straights" would "be quite essential and convenient to a great number of E[astern] Shore Vessels which are compelled to pass through these Straights going & returning, it being the shortest and most convenient route through which the products of a large proportion of the E Shore comes to market."[6]

Thus, both the need for convenient transportation of goods from the rapidly growing farms and towns of the Eastern Shore and concern for the safety of vessels transiting the bay led Congress to appropriate $4,000 for Hooper Strait in the statute of 18 May 1826 which provided for the construction of numerous lighthouses and light boats.

Once Congress had acted, Stephen Pleasonton immediately wrote to William B. Barney, superintendent of lighthouses in Maryland, asking him to advertise for proposals "for a suitable vessel of fifty Ton

Brandywine *was similar to the lightboat stationed in Hooper Strait in 1827, a schooner with a double mast supporting the lamp. Seas seldom ran this high in the strait, but the lightboat was removed from the site during many winters.*

burthen to be fitted in every respect and delivered to her station."[7]

In correspondence Pleasonton usually referred to light vessels as "floating lights." At the end of June he advised Barney that "the Naval Architect...is employed in preparing the draft and description of the Floating Light intended for Hooper Strait."[8]

Unfortunately, no proposals within the budget were received, and Hooper Strait had to wait until 2 March 1827 when Congress passed a second act appropriating an additional $5,000 and increasing the size of the vessel to seventy-two tons.[9]

In July 1827, Barney contracted with William Price of Baltimore to build a "floating light vessel." Price was well-known for his shipbuilding skills, having built several schooners for the navy including *Vixen, Experiment,* and *Hornet*[10] as well as at least seven other schooners, brigs, and ships including the distinguished Baltimore clipper *Nonpareil* (1807).

Price's floating light cost $8,500. She was of white oak and locust, copper and iron fastened, and schooner rigged with two masts. She was sixty-one feet long, sixteen feet of beam, and had a draft of six feet six inches. The illuminating apparatus for the vessel was described as

> ...a double mast in two square pieces of yellow heart pine forty five feet long each answering as ways for the lantern to travel up and down on....The lantern to be fixed upon a frame or carriage of oak...and suspended in equipoise by ropes attached one on each side to the heel of the Carriage close to each piece of the mast, thence passing through the head of each piece over a pulley....The lantern to be drawn down by a single rope as a whip attached to the frame: each piece is to be supported by a pair of shrouds on each side....The frames of the lantern to be made of copper two feet six inches square and three feet six inches high exclusive of its cover or roof, to be glazed with extra panes in each side of white glass of double thickness.
>
> The lamp to be of copper, and of the compass kind fitted to burn twelve wicks and sufficiently large to contain six quarts of oil.[11] [See Appendix 3 for complete contract.]

In the early nineteenth century, keepers won their jobs through political influence. Some of the Hooper Strait keepers were less than qualified, beginning with the first. On 29 October 1827, Pleasonton recommended to President John Quincy Adams that he appoint Richard F. Fox as the first keeper of the Hooper Strait light vessel. In November as the ship was about to go on station on the south side of the channel, Pleasonton notified Barney that Fox had been appointed and should be placed in command of the ship.[12]

In addition to the keeper, the light vessel carried a crew of "three seamen and a boy," each to be paid "wages usually given to seamen and boys in the merchant service...." They were also given twenty-five cents per day in lieu of subsistence with which to defray their expenses, as the captain was to do out of his annual salary of $500.[13]

Superintendent Barney seemed to feel that this crew was inadequate, but Pleasonton assured him that "three men and a boy have on experiment been found sufficient for the Floating Lights in the Chesapeake Bay and no more can be allowed for the one at Hooper's Straits." He added, "No [fire]wood is allowed the Floating Lights within the Bay....They supply themselves by means of their own...boats and the one for Hooper's Straits must adopt the same course."[14]

Records do not show whether Fox immediately took the ship to her station or waited until the spring, but the lightboat, one of the first lighted navigational aids on the Eastern Shore, was in service in 1828. Soon *The American Coast Pilot* by Edmund Blunt, then the chief guide for navigating United States waters, added Hooper Strait to its Chesapeake Bay directions:

> A light vessel has been moored in Hooper's Streights, in 2-1/2 fathoms, necessary to lead vessels clear of the bar off Hooper's Island to the north, and the shoals to the south: it is of service to vessels bound into Tangier Sound.
>
> *Courses to be observed in running into the Streights*
> If from up the bay, bring the light to bear E. by N. and stand for it, which will take you across *Hooper's Island Bar* in about 4 fathoms water. Continue on until you deepen into 7 fathoms, then steer E.N.E. until the light bears E. and run for it. Pass the light on your starboard hand, which will carry you into channel way.
> If from down the bay, bring the light to bear N.E. and steer for it, when you will gradually shoal your water on the south side, you may with safety course round the bar, or shoal in 3 fathoms, until you bring the light to bear E. then steer as above.
> In thick weather, by night or day, a bell will be rung on board the *light vessel* at short intervals, and if thick and blowing, it is ordered to be kept constantly ringing.[15]

Sadly, Keeper Fox turned out to be unreliable. Less than a year later Pleasonton advised Barney to admonish him: "Captain Fox must distinctly understand...that he must not leave the floating light at any time for more than one day without your [Barney's] permission. Should he come to Baltimore again without this permission, it will be recommended to the President to supersede him...."[16] By October 1829, Fox was gone, and the aptly named John Hooper had been appointed in his place.[17]

By 1838, the lantern needed repair. In September Pleasonton wrote to William Frick, superintendent of lights for Maryland, "The lamps ought to be repaired so as to prevent their leaking, and the lantern also ought to be put in good order."[18]

The next spring consideration was given to replacing the lamp completely, but the thrifty Pleasonton decided

> ...the old lantern may be made to answer for some time yet, if he [the keeper] is allowed new rope by which to hoist it to the masthead, as the old ropes are much worn and are in danger of breaking, in which case he would not only be deprived of the use of the lantern, but that there would be great danger that the heavy lead weights by which it is suspended, would fall through both the deck and the bottom of the vessel and sink it.

Pleasonton thereupon directed Frick to supply new ropes as well as new pumps and whatever else was needed "to keep the vessel at her station until the fall when she may be brought into Baltimore and repaired."[19]

John Hooper served as keeper until April 1839. During his command he faced problems caused by storms and ice:

> A schooner of about 40 tons, was discovered within a few yards of the Light-boat...capsized and literally stripped of her sails....She was loaded chiefly with wood, but in part with grain, it is conjectured, as wild fowl have been noticed to flock around her in considerable numbers....Her name is not known, but the word "Snow-Hill" has been discovered painted on her stern. A short time before she is supposed to have foundered, this vessel, it is believed, was seen...riding "like a thing of life," the huge billows of the tempest-lashed sea, and struggling to withstand the furious peltings of the merciless storm, whose strong arm was fraught with calamity to her and, it is feared, death to the whole of her hapless crew.[20]

Ice was a continuing problem for the lightship. In July 1831, Keeper Hooper placed a notice in the Cambridge *Chronicle* that the vessel would be taken to Baltimore for repair of damage caused by ice the previous winter. In December, she was again taken off station due to ice. On that occasion Hooper's notice in the *Chronicle* of 31 December 1831 stated that

> ...the Hooper's Streight Light Boat has been taken off station and carried into harbor. On Saturday, the 17th inst., she was sunk to the

water's edge by ice that made on her bow by the dashing of the waves during the fury of the N. W. gale of that day; and her situation becoming such that she was in great danger of being overwhelmed by floating islands of ice, it was deemed absolutely necessary to run her into a harbor, in order to prevent her total destruction and the loss of those on board.

Later, arguing that the lightship should be taken off station in the winter, Hooper wrote Assistant Superintendent Robert F. Lyons,"Ther is no vessels passing during winter except oyster vessel...;" moreover, "I don't expect that I shall be able to git good men to stay on boar[d] during the winter as so many of the men have experienced the Result of it to there sorrow."[21]

Beginning as early as 1835, lightboat keepers were governed by instructions issued by Pleasonton. Naturally, the keeper's first duty was to "light the lamps every evening at sunsetting, and keep them burning, bright and clear, till sunrising." Lamps and lanterns were to be "constantly kept clean, and in order," and the keeper was to take particular care that "no lamps, wood, or candles are left burning anywhere, so as to endanger fire."

To assure that "the greatest degree of light" was shown at night, "the wicks are to be trimmed every four hours taking care that they are exactly even on top." Other duties of the keeper included keeping "an exact account of the quantity of oil received" and consumed and reporting it quarterly to the superintendent and keeping a daily journal noting absence from the vessel of keeper or crewmembers and the

A U.S. Treasury official, Stephen Pleasonton, ran the lighthouse service from 1820 to 1852. He was famous for his thrift, but American lighthouse technology lagged far behind Europe's during his tenure.

reason why. The keeper was not to absent himself "at any time, without first obtaining the consent of the superintendent."

The lightboat's decks were to be "washed and cleaned at least once a day." The hold was to be rinsed "occasionally" to purify it. "To preserve the vessel from decay" and "promote the health of the crew" during hot months, the hold was to be "well and constantly aired by means of wind-sails." Finally, the ship's ballast was to be "taken up, cleaned, and replaced, every six months."

On the social side, the lightboat keeper was instructed to "treat with civility and attention" strangers visiting the vessel, "not to sell, or permit to be sold, any spirituous liquours on board," nor to employ any "negro or mulatto, whether free or slave...on board the floating light...with the exception of the cook, who may be a person of color."[22]

To what extent these instructions were meticulously followed at Hooper Strait can only be guessed. But even if they were, the lightship had to be repaired in Baltimore in 1835 and again in 1836. Perhaps the latter repair was prompted by Hooper's report that the vessel's "waterways is Rotten & cannot be caulked tite & consequently her beames nees carlins clamps & upper timbers must rot...her standing Riggen is also worn out...." Pleasonton, as usual, tried to pinch pennies. He ordered that the crew be discharged during the repairs since "there would be no difficulty in shipping a new crew in the spring." The Baltimore superintendent thought otherwise since good seamen were hard to find and persuaded Pleasonton to retain the crew.[23]

Although Pleasonton grudgingly authorized laying up the lightship for repairs in 1835 and 1836, he seems to have become reconciled to it by November 1837 when he wrote,

> It appears to be proper that the Hooper Strait Floating Light should be brought into port as soon as there may be indications of hard freezing weather, as her remaining at her station would not only be attended with danger, but would be without advantage to navigation.[24]

This time Pleasonton ordered the crew discharged.

In April 1839, Hooper was replaced by Robert Griffith who was to be the last keeper of the first floating light.[25]

By January 1844, the lightship was again in need of repair. Griffith obtained local estimates of the cost, but after the ship was towed to Baltimore in March, two surveys revealed that she was "not worthy of repair." Nevertheless it was decided to make such temporary repairs as would permit the vessel to return to her station during the summer of 1844 while a new ship could be built.[26] These repairs must have been fairly extensive because in May 1845 Captain H. Prince of the revenue cutter *Madison* reported that the vessel was "clean and well kept" but that she was "moored...about one hundred fathoms too far to the SE." Griffith was directed to place her in the proper position.[27]

More than a year after his 1844 complaint, Griffith again wrote to the new superintendent, William H. Marriott, reminding him that the ship had been surveyed resulting "in the condemnation of Said vessel, as unseaworthy." Griffith also pointed out that he had been informed that the new vessel would be ready by September 1844. Marriott told Pleasonton that "something ought to be done to prevent a withdrawal of the light from the Straits."[28] A contract to construct a new vessel was finally signed in June 1845, but unfortunately Griffith died before the second Hooper Strait light vessel was commissioned.

Second Lightship

The new floating light was constructed by William Easby, a master shipwright at Alexandria, Virginia, then part of the District of Columbia. He had already built a 150-ton revenue cutter, *Walter Forward*, for the government. The contract (Appendix 4) with Easby provided that[29]

> ...in consideration of the sum of *Three thousand five hundred dollars*, lawful money of the United States, the said Wm Easby will forthwith at his own proper cost & expense find & provide all the materials, workmanship & labor, of the best quality, & will well & sufficiently erect, build, finish, complete & fit in a strong & perfect manner, & with good, sound & perfect materials & workmanship, a *Floating* Light vessel, of the burthen of about *Seventy two Tons*, for the Hooper's Straits station, agreeably to a model to be furnished, & of materials corresponding to the following dimensions & specifications, viz;
>
> Length on Deck sixty nine feet,
> Breadth, moulded, seventeen feet six inches,
> Depth of hold, six feet six inches, round of deck seven inches,

> Dead rise to half floor fifteen inches,
> Keel of White oak sided nine inches—twenty inches deep
>   amidships—tapering fore & aft to twelve inches,
> Keelson of White oak, twelve inches by nine inches square....

As further evidence of Pleasonton's parsimony, he left the Hooper Strait station unlighted by sending the old vessel to Washington to transfer its masts, lantern, and other equipment to the new vessel. The new boat was completed at the end of September, and the old floating light went to Alexandria to be auctioned.[30]

At age forty-four Henry Shenton (1804-1873), a native of the Hooper Island area, was appointed the first keeper of the new vessel.[31] He was not beloved by Pleasonton. Soon after his appointment, Pleasonton wrote regarding a disputed account, "It is provoking to have to transact business with a man of so little understanding as Captain Shenton appears to possess."[32]

The new "lead-colored" vessel was equipped with a single light thirty-four feet high and consisting of an oil lamp with eleven cylindrical wicks. Her fog signal comprised a hand-operated bell and horn.

More information about the new ship was given in an 1858 inspection report. The lantern was hoisted by an iron chain runner and weights. Her fog bell weighed between three- and four-hundred pounds. She was moored by one twelve- to fifteen-hundred-pound mushroom anchor and seventy-five fathoms of one-inch chain. A spare four-hundred-pound mushroom and chain were provided. She had two boats, one of seventeen feet, the other fifteen feet, each having a five-foot beam. She could store about three tons of coal on the "birth" deck and about four-hundred gallons of water. Quarters for keeper and crew included four berths in the cabin and four more in the "stearage or birth deck."[33]

Although no official inventory of the cabin furnishings on either of the lightships has been found, when Henry Shenton took his post as first keeper of the new vessel, he listed items he had found on the old boat. The list provides an indication of the frugality of life on board:

> ...oil Cloath for after Cabbin floor, four Chairs, six cups & saucers, six soup plates, six dining plates, six Mettle spoons, six tea spoons, six knives & forks, one Coffee pot, one Coffee boiler, one tin basin, one pitcher, one Coffee mill, two Table Cloaths, four Towels, two pair

small Shovel & tongs, one Sugar box, one Coffee box, half dozen Corn brooms, four Scrubbing brushes, one tea pot, one paper box, Curtins for births in after Cabbin, national flag, three pounds sail twine, half dozen sail nedles, two oars for long boat, Medicine Chest replenished....

Also listed were a quantity of copper nails and tacks, lamp wicks, small hand tools, and "three quires writing paper, one bottle black ink...one funnel and two jugs."[34]

As with the first vessel, winter ice and stormy weather posed problems, and the new ship was sent to Baltimore numerous times for protection from the elements and for repairs.

Pleasonton's difficulties with Shenton resurfaced in December 1847 when Shenton announced plans to take the lightship to Baltimore "at the first opportunity" and had to be directed to remain at his station until permitted to move. Reversing his opinion of 1837, Pleasonton did not want to let Shenton off the hook, adding in his letter, "I am of the opinion, however, that with some thick planks placed about the bows and sides of the vessel, that he might remain at his station all winter for the ice cannot be very dangerous when the vessel is moored."[35]

In 1848 Pleasonton had enough of Shenton. In June he wrote to Superintendent William Cole,

> The account you give of the conduct of the keeper of the floating light at Hooper's Straits is so decidedly bad that I must request you to make inquiry in the neighborhood of that light for a suitable man to take his place....For him and the mate to leave the vessel for days and nights in succession in violation of the Standing Orders of the Department is sufficient cause for removal, but when to this is added that of employing a slave boy at 50 dollars a year and charging and receiving 180 dollars from the United States for him, we should be exceedingly culpable not to put him out of the public service....

Pleasonton said he would call upon Treasury Secretary Robert J. Walker to do so.[36]

George Keene, another Hooper Island area native, succeeded Shenton in April 1849 at age fifty-one.[37] He too was a source of trouble for Pleasonton. In February 1850 Pleasonton asked the secretary to remove the keeper who had "abandoned his station and with his vessel gone into a nearby creek...."[38] However, Keene stayed on the job, probably with the help of political influence. He was still there in November 1850 when a severe gale hit Hooper Strait. Evidently fearing his vessel would capsize from the weight of the lantern aloft, he ordered the mast and lantern posts cut away. Again Pleasonton was angry:

> It appears...that the mast and lantern posts were cut away under the foolish apprehension that the vessel would capsize, and it was owing to that it was necessary to bring the vessel into port and that expensive repairs are required. The Captain of this vessel is certainly not fit for his place and I am strongly inclined to recommend that another be appointed in his place.
>
> The lantern of this vessel was made to run up and down between two strong lantern posts, and if it was found too heavy at the top of the posts in time of high winds, by lowering it down to the deck all danger of capsizing would have been avoided. We have now 40 Floating Lights and many of them have rode out hurricanes without ever having cut away their masts or lantern posts.[39]

Despite this rebuke Keene returned to his station in December. Now he had cause to complain. He reported that the chain attaching the vessel to its mushroom anchor had not been examined for eight years and was now unfit. He requested forty fathoms of chain with a swivel and with shackles every twelve fathoms.[40]

Maintenance practices on the lightboat seem to have been erratic. The anchor chain was not inspected for eight years, and a year passed before a cracked bell was replaced. The vessel was driven ashore in February 1856, and repairs took until July. In the interim the lightship *Relief* took over the station. In 1862 the lantern's glass was broken and had to be replaced, and the same year Keeper Martin L. Wall was ordered to fire Clement Bell because a cook was not an authorized crew member, nor was Wall allowed to employ a slave he owned.[41]

Despite its other problems, the Hooper Strait floating light escaped the fate of most of the Chesapeake Bay lights which were removed, sunk, or destroyed by the Confederates during the Civil War.[42]

Throughout this period keepers frequently changed. Keene finally resigned in 1853 and was succeeded by Severn Mister in January and

Samuel Hardican in May. In 1855 Hardican was replaced by Washington Slocum who resigned in 1857, then by Peter Kirwin who was soon removed and temporarily replaced by the difficult Henry Shenton. Charles V. Crockett was appointed in 1858, then Martin L. Wall in 1861, Joshua Jefferson in 1865, and Zebedee Harper in 1866. Thus over its twenty-two year span, the average tenure of the Hooper Strait lightship's keepers was just two years.

This iron spiral flange, now at the Chesapeake Bay Maritime Museum, was once attached to the bottom of a lighthouse pile. When screwed into sand and clay, it was practically immovable.

However, age was taking its toll on the vessel. In accordance with an 1859 statute, when a lightship needed major overhaul, she was to be replaced by a lighthouse if one could be built on piles at or near the same site.[43] So in 1867 the Light-House Board established a fixed screwpile light station at Hooper Strait. Notice of the change was issued in Baltimore and local newspapers, and in September 1867 the lightship was permanently withdrawn from her station after twenty-two years of mostly efficient service.

Major repairs in 1869 enabled the boat to serve for another eighteen years. She was assigned as relief ship at Deep Water Shoals, Virginia, from 1867 to 1870 and at the Choptank River entrance from 1870 to 1871. From 1872 to 1884 she served at stations in New York and Connecticut where she was stripped and sold at auction for $101.02 in January 1885.[44]

In 1828 Littleton Dennis Teackle had written of the rapidly increasing demand for "the productions of our agriculture, of our valuable forests, and the teeming exuberance of our waters" and of the "constant craving of the western appetite for our delicious oysters." He foresaw that "...in a few years men may see the broad bosom of the Chesapeake, the Mediterranean of the Atlantic Coast, covered with myriads of our fleeting craft, and white with sails from foreign parts...."[45] Teackle would have been proud that the light vessel he fathered had contributed to the safety of those ships and the growth of commerce.

II.
Hooper Strait Lighthouses

By 1867 the Light-House Board under Commodore, later Rear Admiral, William Branford Shubrick (1790-1874) had vastly improved the lighthouse service. Among other things the appointment of keepers had been regularized in an effort to reduce political influence, clearly defined lighthouse districts had been created, and regular inspections of each light station had been scheduled. Many light stations had been added, equipment had been significantly improved, and the Fresnel lens had been introduced widely.

The Fresnel lens is undoubtedly the most important innovation in the history of lighthouses. Its wholesale adoption by the Light-House Board helped bring American lighthouses to the high standard already reached in France and Britain. It was developed by the Frenchman Augustin Fresnel (1788-1827) between 1822 and 1827. Based on his mathematical calculations, he

Commodore William B. Shubrick, U.S. Navy, headed the newly created Light-House Board when the first Hooper Strait lighthouse was built. He endeavored to bring naval standards of professionalism to the service.

17

constructed a series of circular prisms which focused the light emitted by a lighthouse lamp so that it was visible at a much greater distance than that reached by earlier optics and reflectors. Fresnel originally developed four sizes or "orders." They eventually evolved to six modern orders from a first-order, seven-foot ten-inch high giant weighing more than six tons and mainly used for seacoast lighthouses to a two-hundred-twenty-pound sixth-order lens only one foot four inches tall and used in rivers and harbors.[1]

A second important innovation adopted by the Light-House Board was the screwpile support. Invented by English engineer Alexander Mitchell, the screwpile design was first installed at Maplin Sands in the Thames River in 1838. Mitchell's innovation was a spiral-shaped metal disk at the base of a metal bar that made it possible to screw the bar easily into a sand or mud bottom. Besides acting like a screw, the metal disk also provided support for the bar itself since, once in place, it could not be pushed down or pulled up.[2] Several such bars or pilings were connected by cross pieces to form a platform for a lighthouse. The advantages of this type of construction were significant: Construction was relatively inexpensive compared with stone or brick, waves could pass freely between the piles and under the dwelling, and a lighthouse could be put on sandy or muddy bottoms where no suitable base existed for the more traditional stone or brick structure. The design was limited by the type of bottom—rock would not do—and by the depth of water since the pilings could not be very long. Ice could also be a serious problem.

First Lighthouse
Although Stephen Pleasonton grudgingly approved the installation of the first screwpile lighthouse in the United States at Brandywine Shoals, Delaware Bay, in 1848, the Light-House Board recognized their full utility and caused the first Chesapeake Bay screwpile to be erected at Pungoteague Creek, Virginia, in 1854, and the first in Maryland waters

The first screwpile lighthouse was built in England at Maplin Sands in the Thames River where the soft, shifting bottom made conventional masonry construction impossible. The Light-House Board adopted the technology for similar American sites, replacing vessels with buildings on iron piles. ▶

Hooper Strait Lighthouses

Square cottages supported by five pilings were typical of early American screwpile lights. The 1867 Hooper Strait lighthouse probably looked like this; it lasted until 1878, when drifting ice knocked the house off the substructure.

at Sevenfoot Knoll off the Patapsco River in 1855 and 1856. When replacing the deteriorated light vessel at Hooper Strait became essential, the Light-House Board turned to this new design. The Board noted in its annual report for 1867,

> [It is] an object long had in view by the Board, viz., to replace the light-vessels...by permanent structures, because of their greater economy, both in construction and maintenance. Generally, the stations occupied by light-vessels are of such a character that the screw-pile lighthouse is the most eligible form of construction for any permanent substitute. This is particularly the case in the...[Fifth District] owing to the slight elevation of the adjacent shores and their swampy formation, the shallow water and the nature of the bottom.[3]

Work on the first Hooper Strait lighthouse began on 5 August 1867, and the light was "exhibited" or lighted for the first time on the evening of 14 September 1867. It stood on a shoal in six-and-a-half feet of water south of the channel about three-hundred yards southeast of the location of the former light vessel. The iron foundation was painted red, and the superstructure, white.[4]

Although described as a "screwpile," the 1867 lighthouse differed from its successor which is now at the Chesapeake Bay Maritime Museum. It was square, rather than hexagonal, and it stood on five piles, one on each corner of the square and one in the middle. One fender pile

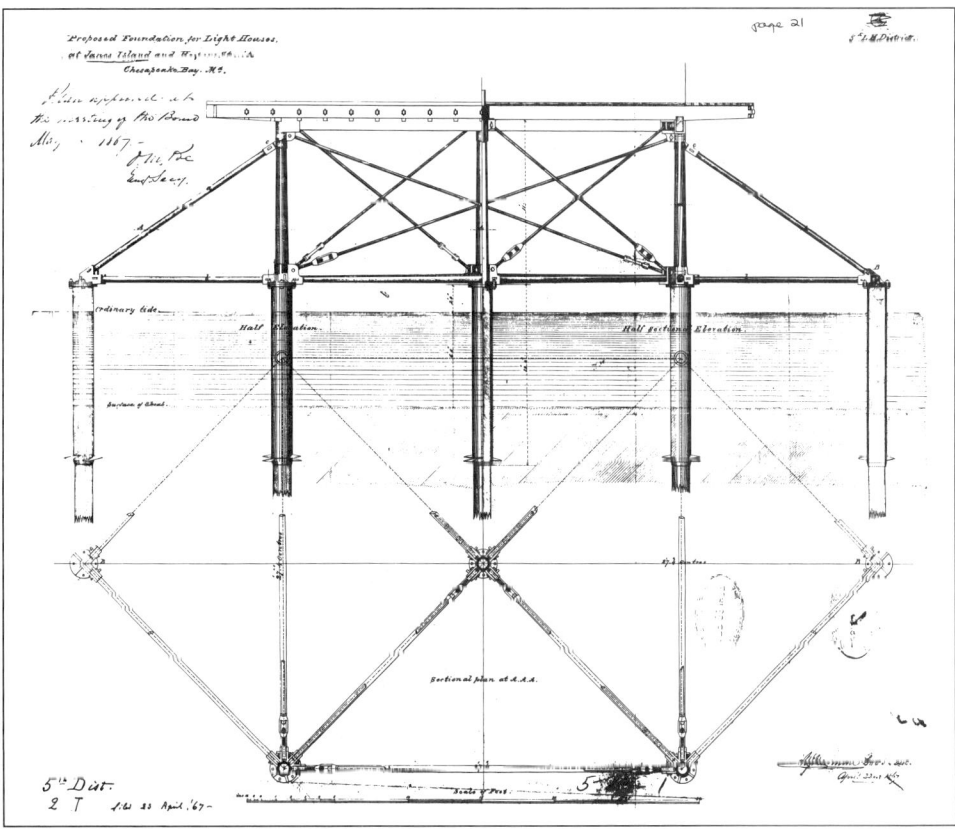

Engineer's drawing for the foundations of the 1867 Hooper Strait and nearby Janes Island lighthouses shows that the screws extended out from iron sleeves which fit over the wooden pilings. Hollow sleeve pilings were later supplanted by stronger solid wrought-iron screw pilings.

stood upstream and one downstream from the foundations. In perhaps the most significant difference, the piles were wood with cast-iron sleeves around them. The wooden piles were driven fifteen to twenty feet into the shoal; the cast-iron sleeves, which had a screw-type flange at the bottom, were screwed about four feet into the shoal and were intended to protect the wooden piles from damage by ice. Although this type of construction may have been cheaper than all-metal piles, the work required was probably greater. As the district engineer observed, "In most cases quite as much power was required to screw down the cast iron sleeve...as to force down the regular screw piles."[5]

By 1871, the new station was equipped with a fog bell in good working order and a fifth-order lens[6] one foot eight inches high and weighing 440 pounds.

Zebedee Harper, the last captain of the lightboat, was the first keeper of the new lighthouse; his assistant was William Meekins. Responsibility for the station was transferred from Baltimore to Crisfield in February 1869.[7]

All went reasonably well until the disastrous winter of 1876-1877. The *Baltimore American and Commercial Advertiser* of 7 January 1877 called it the worst winter in twenty years. As the paper put it, an "ice embargo" commenced on 15 December 1876. In three days twenty-two oystermen were frozen to death or lost; thirty-two lives were lost before the winter was over. The icebreaker *Maryland* had all it could do to keep the Baltimore harbor open. Many sailing vessels were imprisoned in the harbor. On 12 January, twelve to fifteen schooners sank in Annapolis harbor, "being cut through with ice." In the icebound oyster fleet, men killed geese and ducks to keep from starving. Five pungies sank at the mouth of Eastern Bay. Sixty-two vessels were icebound in Eastern Bay for twelve days and had to be rescued by tugs. A police sloop was icebound in St. Michaels harbor.[8]

On Thursday, 11 January, ice in Hooper Strait swept the lighthouse off its foundation and carried it several miles out into the bay. Keeper John Cornwell, who had been appointed in 1869, filed an official report to his superiors in Baltimore eight days after the disaster. His complete

Workmen take test borings of the bay bottom before driving screwpiles. Strata in Hooper Strait ranged from very fine sand at the top through sand and pebbles to solid clay at the bottom. ◀

report stated, "I have the honor to report that the lighthouse at Hooper's Straits was carried away January 11."[9]

At the end of January the *Baltimore American* carried the full story. According to Cornwell's account,

> The ice, carried by the wind and strong current, moved with tremendous force against the light, and although the house fell slowly, he [Cornwell] and his assistant [Alexander S. Conway] were unable to reach their boat. The house filled up with water so that only the roof remained above water, and after great difficulty the boat was floated and a few necessities thrown into it. They were about three miles from the nearest land, and it was determined to row toward it and effect, if possible, a landing on the ice, which extended some distance from the shore. They found, however, that a break would prevent them from reaching land this way. They had, however, drawn the boat on the ice field before the rift was discovered and whilst walking on the ice, he [Conway] fell in the water over his depth, and but for timely assistance must have drowned. The boat had frozen fast to the ice, and chilled through as the men were, they were unable to launch her. Accordingly they laid down in the boat, and unprotected by any covering and exposed to the most chilling cold, they spent twenty-four hours, until Captain Joseph Murphy, of Billup's Island, passing by in his sloop, saw and rescued them. Cornwall's [*sic*] assistant is badly frozen, and a report from Crisfield states that he will hardly recover.[10]

The annual report of the Light-House Board for the year ending 30 June 1877 was more succinct:

> This structure was totally destroyed by ice on January 11, 1877. As soon as the news of its destruction was received, the tenders [*Tulip* and *Heliotrope*] were dispatched to the site, but found the wreck five miles south of Hooper's Straits. The lens, lantern, and other movable articles of property were recovered, when it was found necessary to abandon further attempts at recovery, as the ice was endangering the safety of the vessels. This light-house should be rebuilt, and an appropriation of $20,000 is recommended for the purpose (p. 29).

This was not quite the end of the old lighthouse. Most of the iron foundation remained on site and was deemed a hazard to small boats, so O. E. Maltby of Norfolk was hired to remove it in 1880. The advertisement for bids estimated that fifty-five-thousand pounds of iron were salvageable from Hooper Strait and from the Janes Island lighthouse which had been swept away in January 1879.[11]

Second Lighthouse
As early as 1831 the steamboat *Patuxent* used Hooper Strait as a convenient route to Salisbury and smaller towns on the Wicomico River. By 1877 traffic through the strait had increased with the Eastern Shore Steamboat Company serving the Nanticoke, Pocomoke, and Wicomico Rivers.[12] Thus it is no surprise that petitions calling for rebuilding the lighthouse were received in March and April 1877, though Congress did not appropriate money to rebuild until June 1878. In November preliminary drawings were prepared for a hexagonal house atop a structure of seven splayed wrought-iron pilings,[13] a design that had proved ice-proof at Thomas Point. (The same plans were to be used at Laurel Point, North Carolina, and Janes Island, Maryland.)

Apparently concerned that the new structure should be stronger than the old one, Board Chairman Rear Admiral John Rodgers (1812-1882) queried Fifth District Engineer Orville E. Babcock about the foundations. Babcock replied with a detailed description of pilings, sleeves, and tie-rods.[14] (Appendix 5.)

In December Babcock prepared a cost estimate of $24,035. Later he revised it to an even $20,000, the exact amount Congress had appropriated. The second estimate did not include a lens and fog bell.[15] (Appendix 6.)

Also in 1878 Maryland Governor John Lee Carroll executed two deeds ceding to the United States a five-acre circular plot of

Rear Admiral John Rodgers led the Light-House Board when it approved the building of a new and stronger structure to replace the wrecked 1867 Hooper Strait lighthouse.

submerged land on which the new house would be built.[16] (Appendix 7.) The final site was about 3,500 feet northeast of the old site.

With approval from the Board, Babcock started work on Hooper Strait in January 1879. He hired draughtsman William A. Wansleben to make working drawings which took two months. He ordered North Carolina heart pine for flooring and white pine for joists, beams, and planks from A. A. McCullough of Norfolk and other lumber from Shyrock & Clark of Baltimore. Most of the lumber was delivered to the Lazaretto lighthouse depot in Baltimore.[17]

Baltimore's Smith & King got the contract to supply the millwork (doors and windows) for $293, and Poole & Hunt outbid firms in five other states to win the contract for ironwork. Their low bid was $18,622.27 for all three lighthouses. Poole & Hunt was a large Baltimore foundry and machine works with a long history of building

Poole & Hunt of Baltimore fabricated the wrought-iron substructure for the 1879 lighthouse. They advertised their plant as "unsurpassed facilities for the manufacture of machinery of the largest and heaviest character." They were also the low bidders.

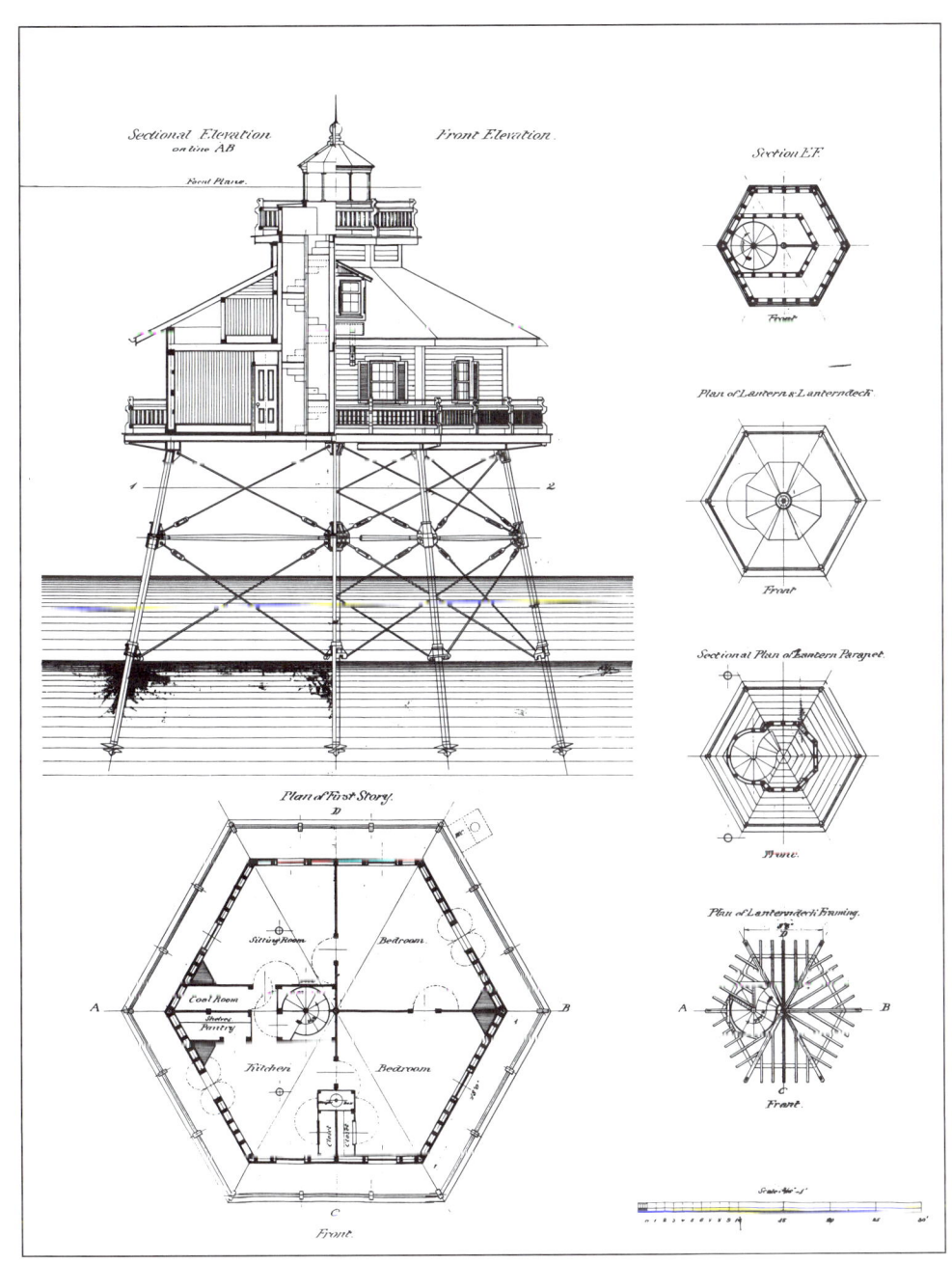

Engineer's drawing shows a cross-section, front elevation, and floor plan of the lighthouse with a circular staircase leading to the lantern. The first floor had a kitchen, sitting room, two bedrooms, coal room, and pantry.

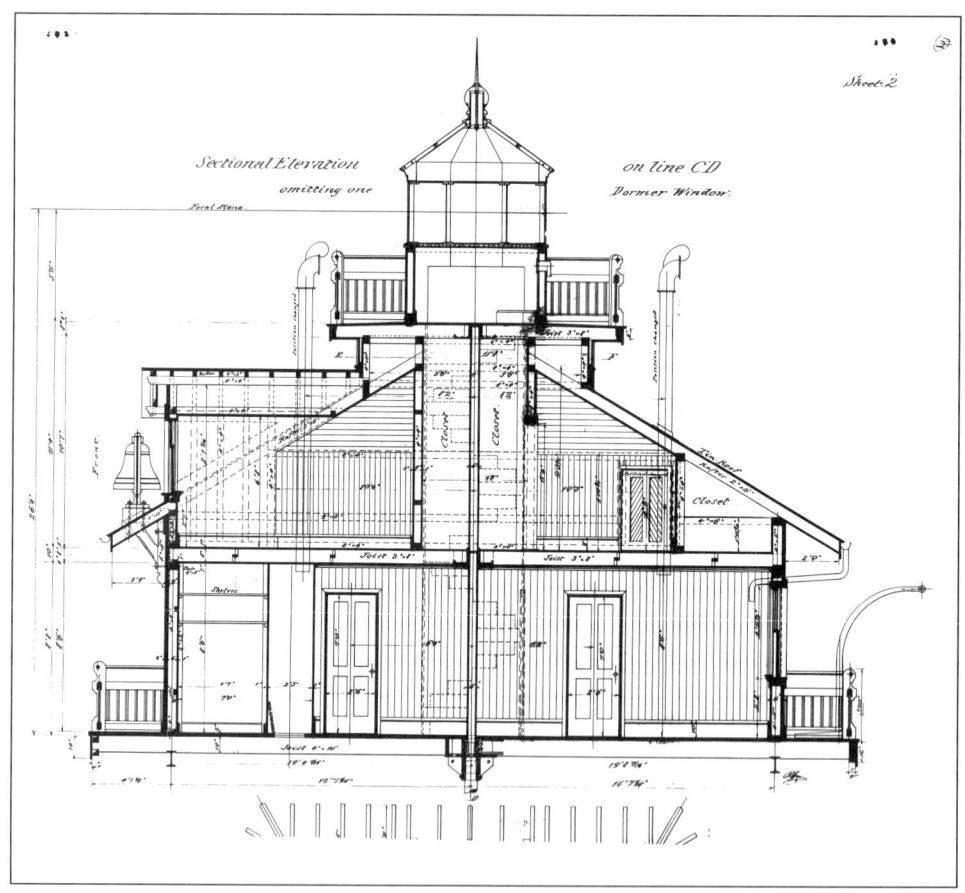

Another cross-section shows one of the two dormers, left. Such plans guided the Lazaretto lighthouse depot carpenters who constructed the building in Baltimore and then took it apart for shipment to Hooper Strait.

boilers, steam engines, machinery, and waterwheels for customers throughout the country. They had made the cast-iron columns for the United States Capitol.[18]

The wooden lighthouse was built at the Lazaretto depot. Finished in June, it was then dismantled for shipping. In August Babcock engaged a schooner from A. J. Hubbard of Fells Point, Baltimore, "...to carry from here all the material for the lighthouses...." The cost was $10 a day, and the crew was expected to load, unload, and "...assist in turning the levers when putting down the screwpiles...."[19]

Work had started on the construction platform by mid-August, when a schooner captain complained to Babcock that no light was displayed "on the construction platform on 19 August and 2 September."[20] Hubbard's schooner took the ironwork and dismantled house to the site, and workers began driving the piles into the sand, pebbles, and clay on 21 September. This presented no difficulties. After the struts, tension braces, and sockets were fitted, the wooden house frame was put in place.

Meanwhile, Babcock was assembling the necessary fittings. He received "five cases and two barrels said to contain supplies and implements for Hooper's Strait L House" from the Third District depot on Staten Island, New York.[21] From the Light-House Board he requisitioned a fifth-order lens made by Barbier and Fenestre of Paris. For the lantern which would surround and protect it, he ordered 3/8-inch thick "French plate glass" from Miguel Aleo of New York City. The cost was $60.75 for the twelve plates,[22] three more than needed for Hooper Strait.

By 9 October everything was ready for installation of the lens, and Babcock visited for a final inspection. On 15 October the fixed white light was shown for the first time.[23]

The Light-House Board was optimistic: "The new structure is expected to withstand the heavy thrust of the ice encountered at this locality. The seven piles upon which the superstructure will rest, are of solid wrought iron, 10 inches in diameter, and... penetrate 25 feet into the shoal."[24]

Despite his previous adventures, John Cornwell accepted the job of keeper; his assistant was Zebedee Harper. Harper's annual salary was $420; Keeper Cornwell's was $540, not too bad at a time when Secretary of the Treasury John Sherman, the overall boss of the lighthouse service, made $8,000.

Lighthouse Routine

Life at the Hooper Strait lighthouse was lonely, partly because the keepers' wives and children were not permitted to live with them, partly because the nearest village, Bishops Head, was over three miles away and difficult to reach by small boat in bad weather. The keeper had an assistant (two or three in later years), and each man could leave the station for eight days a month; otherwise, they were "subject to duty when necessary 24 hours a day." The principal keeper's "first duty [was] to see that the light never fails to burn from sunset to sunrise nor the fog signal to sound when needed. All apparatus required to be kept in perfect condition of cleanliness and operating efficiently and the entire structure thoroughly clean and well painted inside and out."[25]

Keeper William O. Simpkins described his work in the 1920s:

- 25% Painting building including iron work of substructure.
- 15% Handling motor and sail boat alone in all kinds of weather.
- 30% Standing watch six hours each night attending lights and fog signal.
- 10% Routine work such as scrubbing, cleaning, polishing brass, filling lamp.
- 10% Visit two minor lights, painting structures, keeping lanterns in order, these lights six miles from principal station.
- 10% Keeping account of supplies, making reports and correspondence with Superintendents Office. One Asst Keeper under my direction. Going after mail and provisuns ten miles from Station.[26]

The lighthouse was hot in summer, cold in winter, and shook from wakes and seas. Bad weather or good, the keepers were required to follow a specific routine. The ninety-nine page book of *Instructions to Light-Keepers* of July 1881 told them what to do. After lighting the lantern punctually at sunset and keeping it burning at "full intensity until sunrise" when it was extinguished, the keeper must "immediately begin to put the apparatus in order for relighting." Because the lamp burned oil, "...the lens and the glass of the lantern must be cleaned daily...." Special materials had to be prepared and used in cleaning the lens, glass, reflectors, and chimneys, and detailed instructions were given for the process.[27]

The lighthouse was originally equipped with a Steven's Fog Bell Apparatus, and the keepers had to constantly keep it "clean and free from dirt and rust in all its parts." The clockwork mechanism was to be oiled with a "fine oil"—but not too much, "for by that means the machinery and surroundings will become filthy...."

Painting, vitally important in preserving a wood structure, was described in detail. The Light-House Board required certain colors:

Wes Stone, impersonating Keeper George A. Hart, polishes a fifth-order Fresnel lens on display in the Hooper Strait lighthouse. It is similar to the one originally installed there. Manufactured in France, multi-prism Fresnel lenses vastly increased the brilliance and range of the oil-burning lamps

white for the outside of wooden structures, except green for shutters, and brown for ironwork. Inside, all wood "except hardwood" was to be white. The painter was instructed how to prepare wood and metal surfaces and how to mix the paint. The *Instructions* contain a recipe for mixing whitewash and for purifying rainwater: "Put some powdered chalk or whiting into each cistern in which...rain water is collected, and...stir it up well...."[28] In later years pre-mixed paint became available, and between October 1903 and September 1904 the Light-House Board

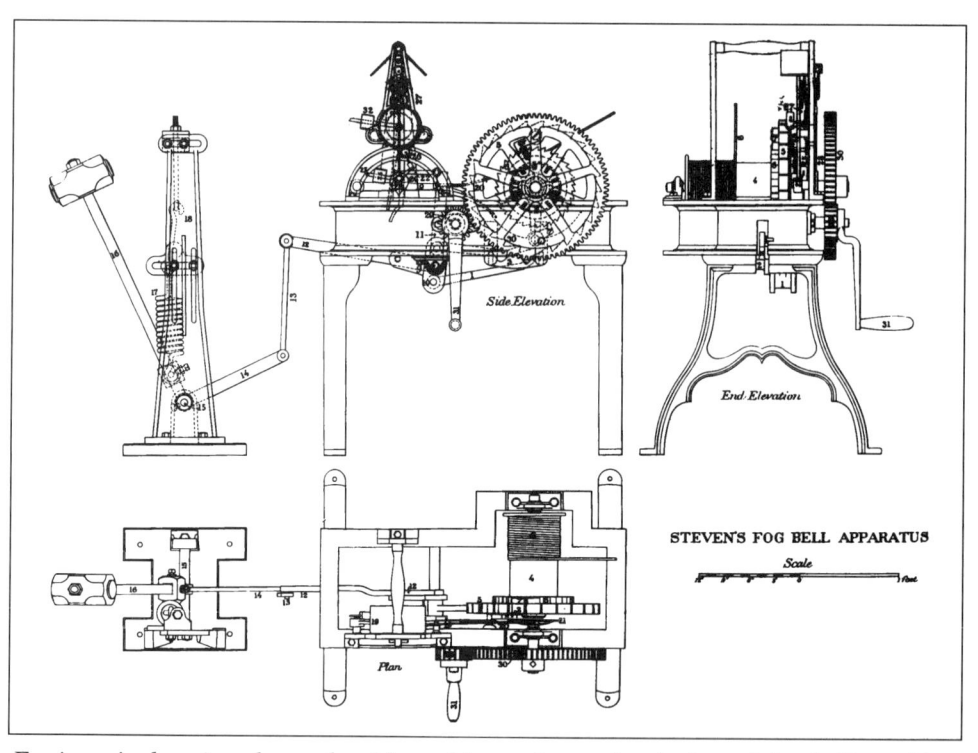

Engineer's drawing shows the side and front views of a clockwork fog bell machine. The hand crank turned the drum (4) to raise the weight attached to the cable wrapped around it. As it descended, the weight (not shown) turned the gears which operated the striking hammer, left.

tender *Holly* delivered at least eighteen gallons of white paint to Hooper Strait.

The instructions also specified the rations to be provided. Each man was annually allowed two-hundred pounds of pork and one hundred of beef, two barrels of flour, fifty pounds of rice, an equal amount of brown sugar, twenty-four pounds of coffee, ten gallons of beans or "pease," four gallons of vinegar, two barrels of potatoes, and a bushel of onions. However, "At the request of the...keeper of the light station, these quantities may be changed, some being increased and others diminished, provided the total cost of the ration is not thereby made greater."

From time to time the monotony was broken by various events: changes in personnel, changes in equipment, bad weather, passing or

Part of the original Hooper Strait fog bell machine is on display in the lighthouse. The rod at left was connected to a hammer which struck a bell once every twelve seconds. Vandals destroyed the timing mechanism.

arriving vessels, and visitors—all reported in the lighthouse log. Miss Fannie Hart and Miss Fannie Kirwin signed the log, and in January 1886 Miss Edna Marsh made her appearance.

On 16 November 1886 a gale blew from the south and southwest. A loaded Baltimore-owned oyster boat went ashore on Hooper's Island, and by the nineteenth it was filled with water, and the owner was stripping it. On 4 January 1887 the strait was so frozen over that the Nanticoke Transportation Company's 126-foot steamer *Nanticoke*, which had passed the light, had to turn back due to the ice, but the new house withstood the ice pressures which had taken out the old one ten years before.

Shortly after the second lighthouse was built, steam sidewheel tender Holly *went into service and supplied all light stations in the bay for fifty years.*

The keepers watched for other traffic. The Oyster Police steamer *Governor Robert M. McLane* was spotted several times in December 1887. In March 1888 she was observed to pass "in and down the sound," and on 2 April Keeper Harper handed his quarterly report to her captain, S. A. Tyler, to mail to the lighthouse inspector. Visits by the lighthouse tenders took place from time to time. On 18 April *Violet* appeared, the lighthouse was inspected, and the small library provided by the Light-House Board was exchanged for a new one. In September the tender *Holly* made several visits.[29]

Tragedy struck twice. On 13 January 1891 his assistant found Keeper Zebedee Harper "spichiles [speechless], he died 5:30 P.M.," having been with the lighthouse service for at least twenty-five years. "Capt Tyler [of the *Governor Robert M. McLane*] come on board and taken him home last night."[30] Keeper Calvin H. Bozeman left his home in Dames Quarter, Maryland, on 4 September 1918, sailed to the lighthouse, and relieved his assistant Ulman Owens, who left for shore. When the crew of a Baltimore, Chesapeake & Atlantic steamer en route through Hooper Strait noticed that the light was not lit a few days later, her captain notified the Baltimore office. On 7 September Bozeman's body was recovered in the strait by the captain of an oyster schooner. The results of an investigation were inconclusive, but Owens surmised that Bozeman, who could not swim, had fallen overboard while sawing wood on a storage platform suspended beneath the lighthouse.[31]

In 1894 George A. Hart of Crapo, Maryland, applied for the keeper's job, stating that he had experience as a sailor, painter, and carpenter. In April Maryland's United States Senator Arthur Poe Gorman wrote the Treasury Secretary that his friends recommended Hart as thoroughly qualified. Although the civil service system had been set up, political connections still had influence in the lighthouse service. In May Treasury appointed Hart acting assistant keeper at Hooper Strait and in September his appointment became permanent. After nearly six years as assistant there and a year and a half as keeper at Sandy Point, Hart returned in 1902 to Hooper Strait as the keeper.[32] He served until 1917.

His tenure was not without problems. One was the difficulty of recruiting and retaining assistants. In March 1904 Hart wrote to his superior, Commander John M. Hawley, the lighthouse inspector at Baltimore, that O. O. Burrus, who had reported for duty on the second, "had got dissatisfied and is going to leave today...." Hart added, "I have a sore hand and am not able to do very much & I have employed Mr. J. R. Jarrett as substitute until you can send me an Asst. which I hope will be soon as I am unwell."[33]

Hart's request was answered promptly. On 26 March R. F. Gaskins reported for duty, but on 4 April he asked for fifteen days leave to get his family "as it is impossible for me to stay here without them." Although leave was granted, on 6 April Hart had to tell the inspector that Gaskins had quit. Gaskins wrote Hawley that he was sorry, but it was impossible for him to stay at the station any longer. He said he wanted to stay until the fifteenth but could not, "for I believe I would nearly lose my mind....It is much lonelier than I thought....I have nothing against the keeper." For his part Hart told Hawley he liked Gaskins and "tried to get him to stay...." He added,

> I do hope that you will send me someone who will stay....I certainly do hate to be having a new man every month and for him to only stay six or seven days. I certainly do everything in my power to make them

satisfied but can not do it....I don't believe any of them fellows from down there will stay here for it is a very lonely place for strangers.[34]

Gaskins was replaced by yet another unhappy assistant, C. H. Fulcher. In July 1904 he asked the inspector to transfer him nearer his home and family in North Carolina. He repeated the request in September asking for transfer to stations at either Roanoke Marshes or Croatan Light, saying, "My parents are old and look to me for help." In October Hart told the inspector that Fulcher had "performed his duties exlent & he fully understands the workings of a light station & I think he will make an excellent keeper in every way." In February 1905 Fulcher pleaded with Commander Henry McCrae, now the inspector at Baltimore, "Please grant me 27 days leaf....I haven't been home Since I first cam in the Servis and my mother being sick would like to see her." In March Fulcher accepted the position of assistant keeper at Roanoke Marshes.[35]

While these frequent changes of personnel might suggest that Hart was a difficult supervisor, one must remember that the Hooper Strait station was in one of the most remote areas of the Eastern Shore. The closest land was Bishops Head, isolated and thinly populated then as it is today and far from transportation or any urban areas. It is easy to see why young men from other parts of the country might find it especially lonely and why the Light-House Board would find it expedient to hire local people such as George Hart as head keepers for such stations.

George Hart was born in Salisbury, Maryland, in November 1862. He lived in the area between Bishops Head and Lakesville, Maryland, probably at Wingate which is about three-and-a-half miles as the crow flies from the Hooper Strait light. He was initially appointed to Hooper Strait as an assistant keeper in 1894. In 1897 he married Fannie Kirwin, undoubtedly the same person who had signed the lighthouse log. The Harts had a large family and continued to live in the area after Hart left the lighthouse service.[36]

Besides his difficulties with assistants, Hart had problems of his own. In June 1905 he asked Inspector McCrae for six days leave because his wife was "real sick," and he could not find anyone to stay with her or take care of the children. Leave was approved. Again in January 1906 Hart received leave because his wife had miscarried and was very ill.

A lighthouse tender approaches the Hooper Strait light as the keeper climbs down to help tie up. Tenders brought food, fuel, equipment, and Coast Guard inspectors who reported any deficiencies.

"She has sent for me today & I have left for home & have left A. Lee Webster in my place," Hart told McCrae. A year later Hart was granted leave again. This time he attached to his request a doctor's certificate that "Millie F. Hart [is] confined to bed from attack of grip and her husband should not leave her at present."[37]

Hart also had trouble with the inspectors. His report to Inspector McCrae in June 1905 speaks for itself:

> Yr letter of 15th stating that it had been reported at yr office that there was no light lit at this station between 12 midnight the 3d & 3 AM the 4th was received yesterday. I will say in reply that I was absent on that date. I left the station on June 1 at 6 PM and returned the 5th at 8 AM which is entered in my Journal and which time I thought I had a right to absent myself without leave from the Inspector. I did not know

anything about the light not burning or the report until the Inspector showed me the letter. So when Mr. Bradford [Hart's assistant] returned I ask him about it....

    Mr. Bradford says he lit the lamp on the night of June 3rd as usual & he visited once or twice & it was alright, the last time he visited about 11 PM and that he came near changing the lamp then but he would wait untill mid. He came down the stairs and sit down in the rocking chair and droped off to sleep and did not know anything more until 3:15 AM of the 4th and he went up to look at the lamp at once. It was still burning but was below the burner so it was not visible & he thought that he would report the matter at once but after thinking over the matter he thought it had only been that way a short while & had not done any particular harm so decided not to say anything about it but says he is very sorry he did not report as it has turned out. I think Mr. Bradford's statement is correct & I am very sorry my self as Mr. Bradford has performed his duties splendid except this case & I hope you may forgive this case....

    PS) So far as the Party says about the light fog I know nothing whatever about it. I do know it never occured when I was here.

No doubt this incident led Hart to tell McCrae in October, "Mr. E. H. Bradford having served six months at this station as Assistant Keeper, I will say that I think that Mr. Bradford will make an average Keeper." McCrae noted, "This is scant praise, but let it go however."[38]

Other personnel problems involved sloppy housekeeping. On 23 February 1907 an inspector reported the station's condition was bad, and by September 1908 it was worse. On the sixth Navy Lieutenant Commander Robert V. Russell, the inspector, wrote in the log,

> Conditions bad both as to repairs and as to order and cleanliness. House dirty and ill-kept. Lamp and lantern panels need cleaning. Book not kept up to date. Station shows evident *neglect* of *duty* on the part of the keepers....Fog Bell out of order. Boats need repairs. Roof of house leaks. Two lantern panels cracked but still serviceable....*Keeper absent.*[39]

Russell was back again on 23 October and reported that conditions were still unsatisfactory, the "lens very dirty (no attempt yet made today to clean it)," and the keeper was again absent without making an entry in the log. Keeper Hart must finally have taken the matter to heart. By 29 December Russell could at last report, "condition very good—a great improvement since last inspection."

Unfortunately, Keeper Hart's career did not end well. For several years he had incurred debts that he had failed to resolve, despite continuing pressure from the Lighthouse Service, and about which he misled the service. He was also absent from his post for long periods, sometimes without permission. In October 1916 he had been absent so long that his assistant, Ulman Owens, wrote the district inspector, "I haven't heard anything from him, it looks like he has left for good."[40]

Though Hart's problems may well have stemmed from the need to provide for his seven children and an ailing wife, nevertheless, on 13 December 1916 the Department of Commerce notified Hart that he was to be removed from his job at the end of the month for false statements, unauthorized absences, unresolved debts, and failure to answer official correspondence promptly.[41]

At the end of 1916 Keeper Hart finally departed, noting in the log, "Good by Old Light House, Geo. A. Hart, Keeper at present." On 1 January 1917 the ill-fated new keeper, Calvin H. Bozeman, took over.[42]

Weather conditions were a frequent subject of letters and log entries. In February 1904 Hart explained a delayed report due to ice, and in February 1907 he did so again:

> Capt. Wm. P. Turley of the Oyster Police Boat set me on board [the lighthouse] on the 4th & the weather became so bad that he would not wait for me to fix up my reports so he could take them ashore & mail them for me so I have been unable to get a shore to mail them on account of wind & ice along the shore until today so beg that you will excuse me of being late..,,[43]

The winter of 1912 was another bad one. The log on 23 January reads, "Ice running very strong. House shaking so bad put light out 5 PM. Ice still running very strong & House shaking very Bad—Can't hardly keep on your feet." By 2 February "Very heavy ice running. House shaking very bad. Can't stand on your feet. 8:30 PM Feb 2 Ice heavier than it ever has been. Shaking House worse. Can't keep lamp lit. 9 PM. Light burning alright, but House still shaking very bad."[44]

Although keepers or their assistants were required to remain at their posts and attend the light and fog bell at all times unless officially relieved, on a few occasions this proved impossible. Between 8 and 15 February 1918 the keeper and assistant "abanded light on account of ice by instructions of Inspector." Keepers had to leave again between 12 and 27 February 1936 and from 27 January to 18 February 1940.[45]

The extent to which wind and waves made the lighthouse vibrate was documented in 1879 by the district engineer in refusing a clock for Hooper Strait: "I have to say that a pendulum clock can be of no value on a screwpile lighthouse where there is more or less vibration from winds, and whenever boats, even small ones, go alongside."[46]

Throughout the great storm of 1933 the keepers stayed on station. The log for 23 August reported that the storm, a gale from the east and south, "wash coal & wood from platform + 20 gallons of gasoline—tore sail up to Sail Boat—Wash away." Other items lost that day included three 10-gallon drums, one 25-gallon drum, several planks, and "1 American flag. Worn out."

Beginning in 1912, Hooper Strait lightkeepers were assigned responsibility for maintaining other aids to navigation: Honga River post light in 1912, Bentleys Point post light in 1928, and Crab Point Bar light in 1930. By 1935 they were required to care for "14 minor lights in the Tar Bay group," some of them about ten miles away. The keepers had to visit these beacons regularly to refill their lanterns with oil. The keeper's salary was increased by $60 to $660, and his assistant's to $540 to cover their new duties.[47]

To take care of these markers, make the nine-mile run to Dames Quarter for supplies, and go ashore for leave, the keepers had two boats at their disposal: a sailboat and, after 1913, a motorboat. Their first gasoline engine was either a Lathrop or a Rapid single-cylinder, four-horsepower engine. Later they received a larger vessel equipped with an eighteen- to twenty-four-horsepower motor that could make seven knots.[48]

During the 1930s the daily dull routine of life in the lighthouse continued. Some of the entries in the log for 1935 are typical: 2 June: "Ran generator No. 1 2 hrs, charged batteries." 5 June: "Varnished engine room floor." 6 June: "Painted Sail boat inside one coat led color." 7 June: "Painted Sail boat outside one coat. Cleaned oil stove."

Post lights like this one supplemented the lighthouses in guiding mariners through twisting channels. Hooper Strait keepers were responsible for fourteen such lights by 1935, refilling them with kerosene once a week and repainting the slats regularly.

8 June: "Cleaned tower, polished lens." 9 June: "Scrubbed kitchen floor." 12 June: "...Started to clean up motor boat and paint motor boat in Side one coat led color and two coat paint outside led color and paint ladder of boat two coats of coffin paint." 21 June: "Scrubbed kitchen. Polished brass...." Sunday, 23 June: "Killing flies."[49]

As for the Hooper Strait light itself, in September 1905 the original red sector, which had been installed in April 1882, was enlarged and an additional sector was installed for the first time.[50] In 1934 the station was electrified, a light bulb replaced the old oil lamp, and an up-to-date air horn replaced the weight-driven fog signal. An estimate of expenses lists the equipment needed: an eight-horsepower gas engine and compressor, a two-hundred-millimeter Tyfon or similar air whistle, two Westinghouse or similar thirty-two-volt generators, twenty-four Edison storage batteries, flashers, operating gear, switchboard, and wiring and installation. The total estimated expense was $2,500. According to the log the new systems were "put in operation" and the generators run on 1 November 1934.[51]

41

The new sixty-watt lamp with a five-hundred-hour life C-5 filament developed thirty-three-hundred candlepower in the white sector and one thousand in the red sector. It flashed every five seconds for one second with a four-second eclipse. The air horn blast was three seconds long with a twelve-second silence between blasts.

The documents do not reveal the decibel level of the air horn, but there is evidence that the keeper was loath to turn it on until absolutely necessary. On 2 November 1936 Captain Webster of the *Red Star*, Victor Lynn line, which served Salisbury, complained that no fog signal was operating at 3 AM and that he was dangerously close to the shoal before he saw the Hooper Strait light. "It was a very close shave that we had." Lighthouse Engineer H. Almy went to Hooper Strait to interview Keeper William O. Simpkins. The keeper showed Almy the log entry which stated that the fog signal had been operating from 3 AM to 8 AM. When asked whether he had heard the *Red Star*, he said that he could not hear anything outside when the signal was going. He said he started the horn when he could not see the nearest land. Almy pointed out that land was only one-and-a-half miles away while the instructions stated that he should start the horn when he could not see five miles. Simpkins was officially reprimanded for waiting too long to sound the fog warning.

William O. Simpkins was keeper at Hooper Strait from 1924 until 1939. His salary was $1,740 a year. He was photographed ashore holding a pair of oyster tongs, probably implying that he had been a waterman.

Almy's visit revealed that Simpkins, a sixteen-year veteran of the lighthouse service, may have acted irregularly in another respect. He was alone at the time of the fog, and Almy noted that "it was evidently the practice at this station for only one man to be on duty...the other two evidently being on leave." Since the station had recently been assigned a second assistant keeper "because it is frequently necessary for 2 men to work together on boat trips to service minor lights,"[52] Almy apparently thought that two men should have been on duty at all times.

On 26 May 1939 communication with the station was brought up to date when the tender delivered a radiotelephone transmitter. It had a thirty-four-foot telescoping antenna on a post inside the lantern gallery railing. The transmitter, receiver, and calling unit were located on the main deck, probably in the kitchen. The cost was approximately $800.[53]

On 1 July 1939 the log noted that the United States Coast Guard had taken over from the Bureau of Lighthouses. This ended thirty-six years of control by the Department of Commerce and, for the first time, combined all coastal navigation and safety activities under one government body. As the Coast Guard assumed control, operational personnel of the former Light House Service were examined to determine their fitness to serve as Coast Guard enlisted men. Thus on 19 December 1939 the log recorded that the tender *Mistletoe* left a quartermaster at the station while Keeper William J. Kelly and one assistant met the Coast Guard Board at Crisfield, Maryland. Kelly passed.

As World War II neared, the tempo of life at the station increased, but only slightly. In June 1941 an additional radio was installed; in July "U.S. Coast Guard" was painted on the motorboat's bow and "Hooper Straits" on its stern. In August a boat loaded with tomatoes ran aground on a bar southeast of the station but floated off an hour later, and in November the 5,832-ton Brazilian steamer *Itamaraty*[54] passed the station outward bound, "the largest ship that ever passed Hooper Strait." There was no comment about the attack on Pearl Harbor on 7 December, but by the seventeenth a continuous listening watch was being maintained on the new radio.[55]

The logs of the Hooper Strait station for the war years 1942 through 1945 reflect the continuing routine of chipping, priming, painting, polishing, scrubbing, and other chores. On 8 May 1942 the cutter *Wisteria* delivered one hundred gallons of gasoline and one hundred gallons of kerosene, and on the twenty-seventh the tender *Violet* delivered a new motorboat and "taken the old motorboat away."[56]

Steam, twin-screw tender Violet *visited Hooper Strait regularly, beginning about 1940. She once delivered a new motorboat to the light station.*

During June and July the crew was busy painting the "post lights" at Windmill Point, Honga River, and Fishing Bay and chipping and painting the ironwork under the lighthouse itself.[57] Occasionally, the war's presence was felt: Without explanation the log for 15 July reported the station was blacked out from 2100 hours until dawn. On 5 August a new lamp was placed in the lighthouse tower, and on 9 December Commander N. C. Manyon inspected the station. Keeper Kelly, First Assistant Harold M. Messick, and J. L. Hughes, Jr., were all aboard and in uniform. Despite the ceremony Commander Manyon did not find everything in proper order. The log contains this entry:

> This Journal must be kept as indicated by instructions on the inside of the front cover. Weather must be recorded every six hours—all lights

sighted at sun down must be recorded in the Book.

Each person on duty must write in the Journal *each* day what he has been doing. This has been called to the attention of the keeper before. Therefore, no further excuses will be accepted.
N. C. Manyon, USCG
9 Dec 42 Aids & Navigation Officer[58]

Following this admonition, the weather was reported as required, and each month the log consumed many more pages than before. On 6 January 1943 the lights visible at sundown were Sharkfin, Holland Island Bar, Great Shoals, Solomons Lump, and Bishops Head. February was cold and wet. On the sixth the fog engine was kept running all day, by the seventeenth the strait was full of ice, and by the nineteenth it was drifting. On 1 March the lamp in the main light burned out at 7:30 PM.

Throughout these years a continuous radio watch was maintained and recorded in the log. No doubt to confuse the enemy, the station's call sign was frequently changed.

The summer of 1943 rolled around, and painting resumed. From the first to the fifteenth of June the crew was engaged in "painting outside of house—all sides." On the eleventh, time was taken "to instruct Personell in artificial Resperation" and to install new radio equipment. Part of July was given over to repairing the rudder and scraping and caulking the sailboat. At 9:00 PM on 22 August the bulb in the main light burned out again but was replaced by 9:30. In preparation for winter, the radiators were drained on the Kohler and fog engines and refilled with Prestone antifreeze on 10 November.

The war was not mentioned again until 6 June 1944 when, next to a small American flag drawn in the margin in red, white, and blue, the log noted,

"D-Day." A Day to be Remembered. Beginning today, Tuesday June 6 1944—3:30 AM The United Allied forces landed on the N.W. coast of France & established a Beach head. There fore opening the Second front in the European Theater of war & by the help of God may this be the beginning of the End of a long Bluddy war which Cost untold millions of inicent lives. And may God help us in this great Campane to free all man Kind, Amen.[59]

Routine continued: 7 June, "shined brass in tower;" 1 July, painted numbers on motorboat; 11 July, "working on inventory;" 16 July, 1st Assistant Cottee "washed clothes, swept floors, mess duty, tested fog signals, and other machinery." On 17 August Keeper Kelly, who apparently had not been well, was replaced by Clyde M. Farrow.[60]

Winter weather was so intense in early 1945 that it began to resemble January 1877 when the first lighthouse was carried away. On 2 February the strait was full of drifting ice. On the third, "...as far as can be seen field of drift ice. No open water anywhere." The next day was worse, "7 PM Heavy ice running Station shaking badly. Have secured lens with rope to keep from falling." On the fifth the "Entire [area?] in vicinity of this unit one solid ice field," on the sixth the strait was "full of heavy drifting ice all day," and on the seventh the strait was "blocked with heavy ice fields...from 3 to 16 inches thick." Once again the new structure proved sturdier than the old and withstood the pressure.

The outside world intruded again in April. On the first the log recorded: "Plane crashed on Bloodsworth Is. 1415 this date. Sent boat to scene. Advised no assistance needed by Navy. Returned to station." 12 April, "President of the U.S. of America died 3:35 PM this date."

The log for 8 May reported with a small American flag, "War in Europe officially declared ended 6:01 PM this 8th day of May 1945." Routine resumed. "18 May, delivered foul weather gear to CG cutter *Hydrangea*, also empty gas drums."

August brought more news. On the fourteenth the log reported that floors were swept, the railing around the station was scrubbed, and, in red ink, "End of Hostilities with Japan officially announced. Ended by the President this 14th day of August 1945 at 1900+15 PM."

By October 1945 the logs had become more formal.[61] A printed format called for a daily weather report, but some latitude was allowed for remarks. These show that life had changed little from prewar days. Arrivals and departures of the uniformed Coast Guard men were recorded, as were the times the light was turned on and off. The round-the-clock radio watch continued, machinery was maintained, and batteries were charged by running the generators.

Few events varied the monotony: In December 1945 the Hooper Island Light Station boat, which had broken down in the bay, was picked up by the freight boat *Southland* of Tangier Island and towed to the

Assistant Keeper William Greenwood was a veteran of the Coast Guard in the stormy North Atlantic when he was appointed to Hooper Strait in 1949. He served until 1951, enjoyed his time there, and said he would like to have spent his retirement in the lighthouse.

Hooper Strait lighthouse with its crew. Later the boat and crew were towed back to their own station by a Coast Guard patrol boat. In January 1946 an inspection found the station in good condition, and in March "one Springfield rifle Model 1903 and one .45 Colt automatic pistol with packing slip inside" were shipped via the Coast Guard cutter *Narcissus* to district headquarters.[62]

Between 1948 and 1954 this rhythm continued. William Greenwood (1928-1991), then a Seaman 1st Class, served at the Hooper Strait Light Station from 1949 to 1951. Years later he recalled the life there for the archives of the Chesapeake Bay Maritime Museum.[63] Two people were on the station at all times. Their duties included turning the light on and off, charging the batteries, and maintaining a radio watch, but seldom receiving any messages. The station had a thirty-two-volt generator, a battery-operated radio, kerosene lamps, and an electric foghorn. Although Greenwood's bedroom was close to the foghorn, he became so used to the noise that it woke him only when it stopped.

One of the five wooden water tanks on which the keepers depended for fresh water. Gutters on the lighthouse roof directed rain into the tank. Keepers scrubbed the roof often, especially before rain, and put chalk in the tank to counteract the poisonous effects of dissolved lead from solder joints.

    The station depended on rainwater and had several large tanks to store it in. Sanitation was served by an outside privy with no door. Coal was used for cooking and heating, and once a month a Coast Guard supply ship from Norfolk visited the station, although food was purchased locally and each man did his own cooking. The station's motorboat was raised and lowered from davits powered by compressed air, and Greenwood remembers taking it to Deal Island once a week for mail and groceries but having to hitchhike the last two miles from the landing place to the Dames Quarter post office.

Greenwood was married and lived in Easton, Maryland. He served three weeks on duty followed by a week off. His family could visit the station but was not allowed to stay overnight.

Recreation consisted of fishing for drum and rockfish. Although "mosquitos ate you up," Greenwood liked living at the lighthouse except perhaps when storm waves broke against the "top of her" or when the navy launched missiles directly over the lighthouse to the target area on nearby Bloodsworth Island. He thought it would have been a good place to retire.

End of an Era
In November 1954 Hooper Strait Light Station was automated, and Keeper George Leikam and his assistants were withdrawn. The last logbook entry, on 29 November, was routine and failed to note that an era was ending.[64] The light station, which had been manned through the administrations of every president from John Quincy Adams to Dwight D. Eisenhower, was turned over to electric control.

The lighthouse remained in service as a navigational aid, unpainted and poorly maintained, until 1966 when the Coast Guard declared it surplus and it was acquired by the Chesapeake Bay Maritime Museum. The museum arranged to have the

The last keeper of the Hooper Strait station was career officer George Leikam (1902-1960). After the lighthouse was automated in November 1954, he transferred to Thomas Point Light, nearer his Baltimore home.

Unmanned, derelict, and vandalized, the lighthouse was declared surplus by the Coast Guard in 1966.

house cut in half horizontally, and each half was taken by barge to the museum grounds on the Miles River at St. Michaels, Maryland, where it was reassembled on new supports and opened to the public in 1967.

The screwpiles remained in place in the waters of Hooper Strait to support the present forty-one-foot high black-and-white structure with diamond-shaped panels. In pristine condition with its lantern again lighted each night, the relocated Hooper Strait lighthouse recalls the years when mariners depended—often for their very lives—on manned lights, and keepers spent lonely days and nights minding their beacons.

The original iron pilings now support a solar-powered flashing light warning mariners of a three-foot shoal on the north side of the strait.

The Chesapeake Bay Maritime Museum moved the lighthouse to St. Michaels in November 1966. It was sliced in two just below the roof, loaded onto a barge (upper left) and towed up the bay (upper right). A crane lifted the sections onto new supports on the museum grounds (left). Volunteers repaired, repainted, and furnished the structure. Today it is the crown jewel of the museum's collection (right), drawing thousands of visitors, some of whom stay overnight and play lighthouse keeper.

Hooper Strait Lighthouses

Appendices

1. Keepers of Lightships and Lighthouses

Name	Date Appointed	Salary
Keepers of the First Lightship		
Richard F. Fox	3 November 1827	$500
John Hooper	16 October 1829	?
Robert Griffith (died)	18 April 1839	500
Keepers of the Second Lightship		
Henry Shenton	11 September 1845	$500
George W. Keene	27 April 1849	500
Severn Mister	25 January 1853	500
Samuel Hardican (removed)	13 May 1853	500
Washington Slocum (resigned)	12 July 1855	500
Peter Kirwin (removed and		500
Henry Shenton, temporarily)	10 March 1857	450
Charles V. Crockett (removed)	13 June 1858	450
Martin L. Wall (removed)	22 May 1861	450
Joshua Jefferson (removed)	1 April 1865	450
Zebedee Harper	27 September 1866	700
Keepers and Assistants of the First Lighthouse		
Zebedee Harper (removed)	11 September 1867	$600
William L. Meekins (Assistant)	11 September 1867	400
John S. Cornwell	21 May 1869	600
Alexander S. Conway (Assistant)	20 July 1869	400

Continued

APPENDIX 1.

Name	Date Appointed	Salary
Keepers and Assistants of the Second Lighthouse		
John S. Cornwell (Acting)	14 October 1879	$540
Zebedee Harper (Acting Assistant)	20 October 1879	420
John S. Cornwell (permanent apptmt)	16 September 1884	540
B. F. Messick (Assistant)	16 September 1884	420
Samuel Snow (declined)	11 September 1885	540
Zebedee Harper	19 November 1885	540
John W. Hastings (Assistant)	16 July 1886	420
William P. Hastings (Assistant)	11 April 1887	420
William D. Elliot (Assistant)	9 April 1890	435
William D. Elliot (Acting)	19 January 1891	575
George E. Wheatley (Assistant)	7 February 1891	435
George E. Wheatley (Acting)	23 April 1894	575
George A. Hart (Assistant)	28 May 1894	435
William K. Slocum	29 November 1898	575
George A. Hart (Assistant)	28 May 1894	435
Albert Olsen (Assistant)	6 June 1900	435
George A. Hart	31 January 1902	575
S. Johnson (Assistant)	1 June 1902	435
Olaf A. Olsen (Assistant)	16 August 1902	435
William J. Moody (Assistant)	1 July 1903	435
O. O. Burrus (Assistant)	2 March 1904	435
J. R. Jarret (Acting Assistant)	10 March 1904	?
R. F. Gaskins (Assistant)	26 March 1904	435
C. H. Fulcher (Assistant)	29 April 1904	435
Ernest L. Bradford (Assistant)	10 April 1905	435
Charles Vette (Assistant)	9 January 1909	40
H. T. McGrath (Assistant)	24 July 1909	40
Ulman Owens (Assistant)	7 September 1911	480
C. H. Bozeman	1 January 1917	?
Ulman Owens (Assistant)	7 September 1911	?
H. T. McGrath	19 September 1918	?
Walter McDorman (Assistant)	19 September 1918	?

Continued

Appendix 1.

Name	Date Appointed	Salary
William O. Simpkins	11 August 1924	$1,740
W. S. Kelly (Assistant)	8 March 1925	1,440
Stephen B. Tillett (Assistant)	26 January 1928	1,440
H. R. Hansberry (Assistant)	12 July 1928	1,440
J. J. Dally (Assistant)	1 December 1928	?
William J. Kelly (Assistant)	6 March 1934	?
John H. McGrath (2d Asst/Temp)	No date	1,440
William J. Kelly	1 July 1939 (?)	1,680
Harold M. Messick (1st Assistant)	1939	1,500
F. A. Massey (2d Assistant)	1941	?
J. L. Hughes, Jr. (later 1st Assistant)	1941	?
C. L. Sadler (2d Assistant)	30 April 1942	?
G. Z. Parks (1st Assistant)	1 January 1943	?
G. F. Cottee (later 1st Assistant)	23 March 1943	?
G. A. Johnson (Mchnsts Mate M 2/c)	2 August 1943	?
D. J. Irwin (Machinists Mate 2/c)	2 August 1943	?
E. R. Gonzalez (Seaman 2/c)	23 February 1944	?
Clyde M. Farrow	17 August 1944	?
L. Hill (Bosun 1/c)	7 November 1944	?
L. H. Huskins (Seaman 1/c)	12 November 1944	?
A. K. Linton	1944	?
U. P. Duchet (Seaman 1/c)	5 October 1945	?
George Leikam	21 October 1945	?
G. F. Cottee (1st Assistant)	23 March 1943	?
K. F. Rossfeld (Seaman 1/c)	18 February 1946	?
Melvin Pugh (Seaman 1/c)	?	?
Nicholas DeRuva (Assistant)	12 December 1947	?
Walter Gray (Bosun's Mate 1/c)	?	?
John R. Bateman (1st Assistant)	1949	?
William C. Greenwood (2d Assistant)	1949	?
R. L. Peters (1st Assistant)	1952	?

Sources: National Archives, Record Group 26, microfilm M1373, roll 2, "List of Appointments of Keepers, 1843-1912;" lighthouse logbooks 1913-1954; and keepers' letters.

APPENDIX 2.

2. Screwpile Lighthouses of Chesapeake Bay

Name	Type	Dates Built
Maryland		
Sevenfoot Knoll	Round	1856
Sharps Island	Hexagonal	1866
Hawkins Point	Square with Tower	1867
Hooper Strait	Square/Hexagonal	1867, 1879
Janes Island	Square/Hexagonal	1867, 1879
Lower Cedar Point	Square	1867, 1896
Somers Cove	Square	1867
Upper Cedar Point	Square	1867
Choptank River	Hexagonal	1871
Love Point	Hexagonal	1872
Solomons Lump	Square	1875
Thomas Point	Hexagonal	1875
Mathias Point	Hexagonal	1876
Drum Point	Hexagonal	1883
Great Shoals	Square	1884
Cobb Point Bar	Square	1889
Holland Island Bar	Hexagonal	1889
Greenbury Point Shoal	Hexagonal	1891
Maryland Point	Hexagonal	1892
Sharkfin Shoal	Hexagonal	1892
Ragged Point	Hexagonal	1910

Continued

Appendix 2.

Name	Type	Dates Built
Virginia		
Pungoteague	?	1854
Deep Water Shoals	Square	1855, 1868
Point of Shoals	Hexagonal	1855
White Shoal	Hexagonal	1855
Stingray Point	Hexagonal	1858
Craney Island	Square/Hexagonal	1859, 1884
Bowlers Rock	?	1868
Smith Point	Hexagonal	1868
Windmill Point	Hexagonal	1869
Wolf Trap	Hexagonal	1870
Lambert Point	?	1872
Thimble Shoals	Square/Hexagonal	1872, 1880
Tue Marshes	Square/Hexagonal	1875
Nansemond River	Hexagonal	1878
Bells Rock	Hexagonal	1881
Old Plantation Flats	Square	1886
Great Wicomico River	Hexagonal	1889
Tangier Sound	Square	1890

Sources: Robert de Gast, *The Lighthouses of the Chesapeake,* and F. Ross Holland, *Maryland Lighthouses.*

3. Transcript of Contract for Construction of First Hooper Strait Lightship

Articles of Agreement made and concluded this fifth day of July in the Year of Our Lord One thousand eight hundred and twenty seven between William B. Barney, Naval Officer for the District of Baltimore in the behalf of the United States of America, of the one part and William Price of the City of Baltimore of the other part— Witnesseth, That the said William Price on his part engaged and agreed to build a floating Light Vessel of the following mentioned description, material, and dimensions and to furnish and equip her in the manner hereinafter prescribed—viz; The principal dimensions are, fifty two feet nine inches, between the perpendiculars; nineteen feet four inches, moulded breadth of Beam; eight feet two inches depth of Hold; measuring seventy two tons and forty four ninety-fifths of a ton, Custom House Measure.

The Keel to be of white Oak, in one piece, sided nine inches, and moulded including the rabbet fourteen inches, parallel all fore and aft having a dead wood nailed on it amidships two inches thick.

The Keelson to be of white oak, sided nine inches and moulded eleven inches. The Stem and Stern posts to be of live oak, sided nine inches and moulded according to the draft. The vessel to be built in frames of live Oak, Locust and red cedar bolted together with two bolts in each Scarf of full three quarter inch iron and to have a full three quarter inch copper bolt driven into every other floor, (the floor timbers to be of white oak), through the Keel and

[2]

and a slack seven eighth inch copper bolt driven through keelson, and every other floor, all to be riveted upon substantial rings of Copper or composition on the underside of the keel; the fastenings of the apron, forward dead-wood, and stern post knee, to be of slack seven eighth copper, as high as seven feet nine inches above the bottom of the Keel, and above that they will be of seven eighth inch iron. The floors will be sided seven inches and moulded in the throat eight inches at ribbon six and a half inches and thence by a diminishing line; The futtocks etc. will be moulded to four inches at the deck and thence to three and three quarters at the rail. The first futtock will be sided six and a half inches Second ditto six inches and

Appendix 3.

the top timbers etc. sided four inches. The wales to be of white oak, in two strakes seven inches under each and three inches thick reducing each strake below one quarter of an inch until they compare with the bottom plank which will be full two inches when worked of white oak and be dubbed off flush—no strake below the floor heads to be more than eleven inches nor any one above them to be more than nine inches wide. The fastenings of the bottom to be of copper spikes as high as the heads amidships and thence by a straight line fore and aft &, above that line, of iron, all to be in length twice and one half the thickness of the plank through which they are driven, two spikes to go through each strake into each timber of each frame square fastened and no tree nails; those of the ceiling which will be two inch oak—plank will be of iron of same length as on the outside one spike in each timber of each frame cross fastened to be butt-bolted with slack three quarter inch Copper and the bolts to be rivetted on composition rings. The beams to be of yellow heart pine or of good white oak free from sap sided ten and moulded nine inches to spring fifteen inches in nineteen feet, kneed at each end with two tap knees, excepting the four beams amidships each of which will have a lodge and a dagger knee fazed at each end, all to be sided six inches and bolted with slack seven eighths iron, except one bolt near the end of the body of each dagger which will be of copper of that size; the upper sides of beams will be kept seven and a half inches above the clamps, so that the bolts through the knees may pass through the beams about midway between their upper and lower sides, as also to give air to the deck the arms of the knees to be not less than three feet nine inches long and the bodies of the daggers not less than five feet six inches, the bolts all to be rivetted on rings. The lodges to be of heart yellow pine free from sap, large knots and other defects sided four inches and moulded five and half. The Deck-plank to be of heart-yellow pine free from sap, large knots and other defects, full two inches thick when marked and in strakes not more than eight inches wide fastened with five inch copper spikes, well punched in and plugged

[3]

plugged, and after the Deck is dubbed off, caulked, and planed to be well varnished. To have two Stern hooks and three breast hooks all sided nine inches except the one through which the mooring ring bolt goes which will be sided ten inches, all bolted with slack seven eighth

Appendix 3.

inch copper below and same dimensions iron above the copper fastenings. There will be a list (?) of four inches in width left out all fore and aft at the lower edge of the strake below the clamps for the purpose of giving air. To have a plank shear, water way, let over stauncheons running up at every other frame upon the tops of which there will be fazed a solid rail of oak or heart-yellow-pine three and a quarter inches thick and five and a half inches wide let down half an inch upon the heads of the Stauncheons and fastened with stay-nails, the waist being left open all fore and aft. She will be coppered with twenty four ounce copper as high abaft as eight feet and forward as seven feet six inches above the bottom of the Keel and thence by a straight line fore and aft. To have a trunk cabin fitted for the accommodation of six persons with berths, lockers, cupboards etc. complete. To have a double mast in two square pieces of yellow heart pine forty five feet long each answering as ways for the lantern to travel up and down on or between and kept about three feet four inches apart—in the clear fore and aft-wise for that purpose. The lantern to be fixed upon a frame or carriage of oak (as per draft) and suspended in equipoise by ropes attached one on each side to the heel of the Carriage close to each piece of the mast, thence passing through the head of each piece over a pulley or sheave are fastened to leaden weights traversing in grooves formed by battens nailed on the forward and after sides of the forward and after pieces of this double mast, the forward and after pieces each to be eleven inches square exclusive of the battens which form the grooves for the weights to travel in. The lantern to be drawn down by a single rope as a whip attached to the frame: each piece is to be supported by a pair of shrouds on each side of five inch rope over its head. The aftermost shrouds to lead well aft and a five inch stay from the head of the foremost mast-piece to lead forward to the end of the bowsprit which will be about five feet outboard. These mast-pieces are kept in their parallel directions by a flat iron hexagonal hoop three inches broad and five eighths of an inch thick embracing a square headed collar bolt one and a quarter inch diameter in the head of the centre of each mast-piece over which after the pieces are rigged the hoop is placed and firmly keyed down. This hoop is open sufficiently for the lantern to pass through it with facility. The frames of the lantern to be made of copper two feet six inches square and three feet six inches high exclusive of its cover or roof, to be glazed with extra panes in each side of white glass of double thickness. The lamp to

Appendix 3.

[4]

to be of copper, and of the compass kind fitted to burn twelve wicks and sufficiently large to contain six quarts of oil. To have a trysail-mast a boom and gaft and a Conductor or lightning-rod of half inch iron with a spindle reaching two feet above the lantern, the end of which for one foot down to be well covered with gold leaf and the lower end of the rod to extend eight feet into the water—A Camboose of sufficient size to accommodate six persons, secured either upon deck or in the hold as may be most convenient according to the season of the year upon a platform covered with thick sheet-lead.—To have two good pumps with boxes etc. complete. To have a bell of the usual material of two hundred pounds weight well hung within a strong belfry.—Twenty five tons of Kentledge kept two inches from the ceiling by battens and covered over by a platform or flooring of inch and a half heart pine plank laid upon straight sleepers or beams of heart yellow-pine six inches square to be well and properly secured.—A mushroom anchor of twelve hundred pounds weight having a cast iron head and wrought iron shank and a kedge-anchor of the usual form of seven hundred pounds weight—a chain-cable of inch and quarter iron, sixty fathoms long of the best proven quality, and a nine inch hempen cable of eighty fathoms of best hemp. One boat, sixteen feet long, with rudder, tiller, four oars, one boat-hook and eye and ring bolts complete—to be painted over inside and out with two coats best paint exclusive of priming.—Of the Mooring-ring-bolt to which the chain-cable is to be attached by a shackle the eye will be formed with a solid throat piece and of two and a half inch tough iron, to hold the same size four inches within the stem where the bolt will be reduced to two inches, be well driven, and having a screw cut on its end will be secured with a good strong burr or nut having one or more substantial rings or washers under it—The ring to be of two and a half inch iron and five inches in the clear. There will be a plate of iron let into the stem on each side long enough for a rivet above and one below the ring-bolt of three quarter inch iron well rivetted to secure the stem from splitting. To have a bulkhead forward of the mast forming an oil-room which is to be properly floored for that purpose and furnished with eight tanks or cisterns of fifty gallons each made of double tin with covers, brass casks, and proper stands. To have a storm mainsail and a jib of No. 1 Canvass, and an awning of the best Canvass to extend from the stern to the mast, with all the requisites for furling or

APPENDIX 3.

spreading the same. A sufficient deck-tackle fall and blocks, etc. for weighing the anchors etc. and all the rigging, etc. necessary for raising and securing the sails & lantern, boat etc. etc. Two sixty gallon and four thirty gallon iron bound water casks, four buckets, two harness casks, etc. and a suitable cast iron stove for the cabin with pipe etc. complete. A rudder and Tiller of proper materials and dimensions; the fastenings to

[5]

to correspond with the fastenings already prescribed for the hull of the vessel. The vessel to be painted above the copper over the rail and one strake upon deck as also the cabin and all other parts usually painted with three coats of good paint including the priming, of the color usually employed. Also the materials to be of the best quality and the vessel with all her fixtures and equipment to be finished in the most complete and workmanlike manner to the entire satisfaction of the aforesaid contracting agent of the United States or to the satisfaction of such person as he may appoint to examine the same and to be delivered to the aforesaid Agent on or before the first day of November next. The Contractor to conform in all respects to the plan or draft furnished him by the aforesaid contracting Agent of the Government.

And the said William Price agreed and engaged to furnish all the requisite materials for the building, equipping and furnishing the said Light-vessel, and to do all the aforesaid work in a faithful and workman-like manner on or before the first day of November next for the consideration. . . . . of Eight Thousand, Five Hundred Dollars.

And the said William B. Barney in his aforesaid capacity agreed and engaged on his part to pay to the said William Price the aforesaid sum of Eight-Thousand, Five Hundred Dollars, when the said Light-vessel with all her fixtures and equipment, is completed approved and delivered in conformity with the foregoing agreement.

It is hereby provided that no member of Congress shall be admitted to any share or part of this Contract or agreement or to any benefit to arise therefrom.

Appendix 3.

(signed)
William Price (seal)

William B. Barney (seal)
Sealed and delivered in the presence of

(sd)
J. Mosher

Baltimore, July 7th 1828

I hereby certify, I superintended the building of the Light Boat for Hooper's Straits from the laying of the Keel until her being completed and that she was built agreeably to the Contract made with W. Price and in fact had considerable additional work not called for in the Contract.

(signed)
Ezekiel Jones

Note: Numbers in brackets refer to page numbers of original.

Source: National Archives, Record Group 26, Deeds and Contracts, vol. E. (1825-1834), 20-24. Photocopy of original received from John Earle, date unknown. Transcript from photocopy prepared 1 May 1996 by author and compared with original at National Archives on 29 May 1996.

APPENDIX 4.

4. Transcript of Contract for Construction of Second Hooper Strait Lightship (1845)

[379]

Contract with Capt. W. Easby, for building a new Light Boat for Hooper's Straits, Chesapeake Bay. June 12, 1845

This contract made & entered into this twelfth day of June, one thousand eight hundred & forty five, between William Easby of the City of Washington, master Shipwright, of the one part, & Wm. H. Marriott, Superintendent of Lights for the District of Baltimore, acting for & on behalf of the Secretary of the Treasury of the United States, agreeably to instructions received from Stephen Pleasonton, Esqr., 5th Auditor of the Treasury Department dated 5th June 1845, of the other part, Witnesseth —

That the said William Easby doth hereby contract & engage with the said Wm. H. Marriott as follows, that the said Wm. Easby in consideration of the sum of Three thousand five hundred dollars, lawful money of the United States, will forthwith at his own proper cost & expense find & provide all the materials, workmanship & labor, of the best quality, & will well & sufficiently erect, build, finish, complete & fit in a strong & perfect manner, & with good, sound & perfect materials & workmanship, a Floating Light vessel, of the burthen of about Seventy two Tons, for the Hooper's Straits station, agreeably to a model to be furnished, & of materials corresponding to the following dimensions & specifications, viz;

Length on Deck sixty nine feet,
Breadth, moulded, seventeen feet six inches,
Depth of hold, six feet six inches, round of deck seven inches,
Dead (?) rise to half floor fifteen inches,
Keel of White oak sided nine inches—twenty inches deep amidships—tapering fore & aft to twelve inches,
Keelson of White oak, twelve inches by nine inches square,

[380]

Appendix 4.

Deck wood forward & aft of live oak or locust to side nine inches—to be bolted with copper three quarters of an inch diameter,

Stern Post knee of live oak, bolted with copper 3/4 of an inch in diameter, three bolts in the body & three in the arm, to be rivited under the keel on the aft side of the stern post.

The main & inner stern post of live oak or locust to side nine inches,

Apron of live oak or locust to side eleven inches—bolted with copper, 3/4 of an inch in diameter,

Floor timbers of white oak to mould eight inches at the floor heads, the footlocks (?) & top timbers of live oak, locust or red cedar, to mould five inches at the plank shear—to be completely framed & bolted with iron, every other floor timber to be bolted through the Keel with copper 3/4 of an inch in diameter,

The alternate floor timbers to be bolted after the Keelson is fitted with copper bolts of the same diameter riveted under the Keel,

The main transom or hook of live oak or locust bolted with two copper bolts to the stern post—of 3/4 of an inch in diameter, two hooks are required forward & aft secured with seven copper bolts in each hook of 3/4 of an inch in diameter, the Knight heads & hawse pieces of live oak or locust to side eight inches,

The Wales, four in number, three inches thick, about seven inches wide, fairly & gradually diminished to the bottom plank of two & a half inches thick of white oak, to be fastened with three copper or composition spikes of six inches in length & one copper bolt of 5/8 of an inch in diameter driven through & riveted on the inside of each frame on the ceiling or clamp comprising the two timbers—& from the wales to the keel the bottom planks to be fastened in the same manner;

No treenails to be used;

Butt & flooders (?) end (?) bolts of copper 3/4 of an inch in diameter;

Two chain plates to be fitted on each side;

Plank shear of yellow pine, three inches thick plugged;

A stancheon to every frame, of locust if required;

An open waiste (?) of yellow pine one inch in thickness,

The clamps of yellow pine six by twelve inches square, & four diagonal white oak knees on each side, fastened with copper bolts through the side, 3/4 of an inch in diameter;

Beams of heart yellow pine or white oak, four feet assunder—

Appendix 4.

moulded six sided—ten inches;

The Bowsprit ten feet outboard, & sixteen inches in diameter,

The masts double, forty five feet long, twelve inches square & 3 feet

[381]

feet apart—fore & aft—of heart yellow pine,

The deck planks of white pine—three inches thick—fastened with iron spikes & plugged;

The ceiling plank of yellow pine two inches thick, fastened with iron; the berth deck plank of yellow pine two inches thick; the Cat Heads of white oak;

Salt stops to be placed fore & aft 18 inches below the plank shear,

Four cranes for the quarter Boats are required, & a Capstan or Windlass of sufficient size for the accomodation of six persons—with a platform covered with zinc. Two common pumps are required;

The Oakum in the wales & bottom planks is to be haused to about half an inch of the inner edge of the seams;

The vessel is to be coppered to about one foot above lead water line—with 24 oz. copper;

A trunk cabin to finished with seasoned white pine—furnished with berths, Lockers, & sleves (?) for six persons;

A Bulkhead fixed forward of the foremast forming a room large enough to contain eight double tin cannisters of fifty gallons each;

Battens are to be placed on the ceiling to keep the ballast two inches above the planks;

The arrangement of the Deck & Trunk of Cabin, together with the hawse pipes, Windless bitts, hatchways, scuttles, skylights, gangway ladders, cavils, cleats, & deck bolts to be completed & placed as may be directed;

The vessel to be built at the City of Washington, to be completely painted inboard & out board with three coats of good paint, to be completed to the satisfaction of the said William H. Marriot, or such person as he shall appoint to examine & approve of the materials & superintend the work as it progresses, & delivered at Baltimore on or before the 1st day of October next, & before any payment shall be made under this contract.

In consideration of the due & full performance by the said William Easby of what is hereinbefore agreed to be done by the said

APPENDIX 4.

William Easby, the said William H. Marriott, Superintendent of Lights for the District of Baltimore, acting for & in behalf of the Secretary of the Treasury of the United States, doth hereby agree to pay to the said Wm. Easby the above sum of Three thousand & five hundred dollars, on his producing a Certificate from the person appointed or to be appointed by the said William H. Marriott, that the materials of said vessel are approved of, & the work on said vessel has been satisfactorily done,

[382]

and the vessel delivered in Baltimore.

In witness whereof each of the said parties have hereunto interchangeably set their hands & seals the day & year first hereinbefore written.

Wm Easby (seal)

Wm H. Marriott (seal)
Signed, sealed & delivered in presence of
 Ashbel Steele
 Henry W. Ball, Jr
 John C. Van Wyck

Source: National Archives, Record Group 26, Deeds and Contracts, vol. G (1839-1847), 379-382.

Numbers in brackets refer to page numbers of the contract in bound volume G.

APPENDIX 5.

5. Description of the Foundations for the Second Hooper Strait Lighthouse

The foundations of the house will consist of seven screwpiles disposed in the form of a regular hexagonal polygon with a pile in the center, the other piles to be inclined, the center pile to be perpendicular, all to made of wrought iron ten (10) inches in diameter and to be provided with cast iron screws three (3) feet in diameter.

The piles will be capped by cast iron sleeves with sockets to receive the wrought iron columns or pillars seven (7) inches in diameter.

The caps are provided with flanges to receive the periphery struts. The latter are to be round, 6-1/2 inches in diameter [illegible] tapering to 5-1/2 inches at the ends. They are held in the flanges by means of wrought-iron pins.

All the castings are provided with a series of smaller flanges for the tie-rods.

The sleeve castings are held in position by collars forged to the foundation piles and are provided with hooks for the attachment of the lower tie-rods.

The tie-rods to be of wrought iron, two (2) inches in diameter, made in two parts, connected by means of turnbuckles.

The periphery I beams nine (9) inches high by five and three eighths (5-3/8) inches wide and five eighths (5/8) of an inch thick (?) are bolted to the cap castings of the columns.

Six (6) radial I beams, resting on the cap castings, will form the decking for the house and will be nine (9) inches high, five and three eighths (5-3/8) inches wide and 5/8 of an inch thick.

Channel irons nine (9) inches high by five and three-fourths (5-3/4) inches wide will be attached to the outside of the radial I beams by means of [illegible] plates.

There will be two (2) sets of ladders at the [illegible] pattern, provided with platforms at the height of the [illegible].

Source: National Archives, Record Group 26, "Records of the 5th Lighthouse District," NC 63, entry 3; National Archives, Record Group 26, "Field Records of the Lighthouse Board and Bureau, Records of the 5th District," Baltimore, NC 63, entry 3, vol. 378, 384, Babcock to Rodgers, 6 December 1878.

APPENDIX 6.

6. Engineer's Estimates of Cost of Second Hooper Strait Lighthouse

First Estimate, 11 December 1878

Iron Work	$10,650.00
Lumber	3,000.00
Labor	5,830.00
Paint, Oil, Glass, etc.	350.00
Hardware	475.00
Tin Work	300.00
Fog Bell, etc.	650.00
Boats	360.00
Lens	1,100.00
Provisions	900.00
Freight	200.00
Rope	100.00
Stoves, Wood and Fixtures	100.00
Total	$24,035.00 [sic]

Revised Estimate, 13 January 1879

Iron Work	$9,000.00
Lumber	2,700.00
Labor	5,380.00
Paint, Oil, Glass, etc.	350.00
Hardware	475.00
Tin Work	300.00
Boats	360.00
Provisions	700.00
Freight, etc.	200.00
Rope	120.00
Stoves and Fixtures	100.00
Incidentals	65.00
Total	$20,000.00 [sic]

Source: National Archives, Record Group 26, "Records of the 5th Lighthouse District," NC 63, entry 3, "Field Records of the Lighthouse Board and Bureau, Records of the 5th District," Baltimore, NC 63, entry 3, vol. 378, 420-1 and 468-9, Babcock to Rodgers, 11 December 1878 and 13 January 1879.

APPENDIX 7.

7. Description of Property Ceded to the United States by Governor of Maryland for Second Hooper Strait Lighthouse

Governor John Lee Carroll executed two deeds to the United States for submerged land in Hooper Strait on which to erect the second lighthouse. The first deed, dated 16 February 1878, conveyed the following property:

> Whereas application has been made by a duly authorized agent of the United States describing the site required for a Light-house known as Hoopers Straights Light-house, situated on the east side of Chesapeake Bay on the shoal south side of the channel between Hooper's and Bloodsworth Islands and abreast of entrance to Honga River, Dorchester County, Maryland; said site to contain five (5) acres of land within a circle whose centre, marked A on the accompanying plan is distant four and three-eighth (4 3/8) nautical miles E. by S. 3/4 S. from Richland Point, Hooper's Island, and two and three-eighths (2 3/8) nautical miles S. by W. 1/4 W. from Norman's Cove and which has according to the Coast Survey Chart of 1872, Latitude 38° 12' 57" N. and Longitude 76° 04' 48" W. and whose circumfrence or boundary line shall be two hundred and sixty-three and two tenths (263.2) feet from the centre in every direction.

Governor Carroll's second deed is dated 12 December 1878 and ceded property described as follows:

> Five (5) acres of land situated on the East side of Chesapeake Bay, on the shoal North side of the channel between the mainland (called Bishops Head) and Bloodsworth Island, Dorchester County, Maryland, distant W. 1/2 S. four and a half (4-1/2) nautical miles from Clay Island Light House and S. by E. one and three quarters (1 3/4) nautical miles from Norman's Cove, and which has, according to Coast Survey Chart No. 34, of Chesapeake Bay, 1872, Latitude 38° 13' (32") N. and Longitude 76° 03' (47") W. and whose circumfrence or boundary line shall be 263.3 feet from the centre in every direction.

According to the *List of Lights and Fog Signals on the Atlantic and Gulf Coasts* of 1 March 1905 (Government Printing Office, Washington, 1905), the actual location of the lighthouse was at latitude 38° 13'

Appendix 7.

36" N. and longitude 76° 04' 33" W. Thus, the first deed placed the site on the south side of the channel; the second deed moved the site to the north side of the channel, 46" (about 0.8 miles) east of its true, final location.

Sources: Both deeds are in the Dorchester County Land Records; the first at Liber F. J. H. 12, folios 92-94; the second in Liber F. J. H. 13, folios 501-502. The National Archives, Lighthouse Site File, Hooper Strait, RG 26, Entry 66, contains letters requesting cession of the property and approvals by the U.S. Attorney General.

Notes

Abbreviations Used in Notes

COR NA, RG 26, entry 50, "Correspondence," fldr. 2104.

FR NA, RG 26, "Field Records of the Light-House Board and Bureau, Records of the 5th District," Baltimore, NC 63, entry 3.

FRL NA, RG 26, "Field Records of the Light-House Board and Bureau, Records of the 5th District, 1851-1912," Baltimore, NC 63, entry 3: This series of records consists mainly of letters from keepers in the 5th district to the inspector at Baltimore.

LFS NA, RG 26, "Lighthouse Letters Received from Lighthouse Superintendents 1803-1852, Baltimore, 1825-1852," boxes 1 and 9, entry 17C, NC 31. This series includes letters superintendents received from keepers and forwarded to Pleasonton.

LHL-HS NA, RG 26, "Lighthouse Logs—Hooper Strait."

LSA NA, RG 26, "Letters Sent by the 5th Auditor of the Treasury Department of the United States Regarding the Lighthouse Service." The LSA comprise thirty-one volumes from 1820 to 1853.

NA National Archives

NPRC National Personnel Records Center

RG Record Group

NOTES TO PART I.

I. Hooper Strait Lightships

1. For general background on the history of American marine navigation aids, see: Robert Erwin Johnson, *Guardians of the Sea* (Annapolis: Naval Institute Press, 1987); Robert de Gast, *The Lighthouses of the Chesapeake* (Baltimore: Johns Hopkins University Press, 1973); Ross Holland, *Maryland Lighthouses of the Chesapeake Bay* (Crownsville and Colton Point, Maryland: The Maryland Historical Trust Press, 1997); Dennis L. Noble, *Lighthouses & Keepers* (Annapolis: Naval Institute Press, 1997); and NA, "Introduction to Inventory of Record Group 26."

2. NA, Legislative Division, Petitions and Memorials Referred to the Commerce Committee, House of Representatives, HR 19A, G3.1.

3. Ibid.

4. Ibid. In addition to petitions and letters this file contains the General Assembly's resolution and the governor's transmittal dated 18 February 1826. The resolution, No. 31, is also in *Laws Made and Passed by the Assembly, 1825* (Annapolis: J. Hughes, 1825), 241. The resolution furthers, "An Act to provide for the cession of territorial jurisdiction at Cedar Point, and at Point Look Out in St. Marys county, and at Smiths Island in Cajeys [Kedges] Streights in Somerset County for the erection of light houses thereon," *Laws,* Chapter 169:129.

5. Fielding Lucas, Jr., *A Chart of the Chesapeake and Delaware Bays, 1832,* figs. 62 and 65 in Edward C. Papenfuse and Joseph M. Coale III, *The Hammond-Harwood House Atlas of Historical Maps of Maryland, 1608-1908* (Baltimore: Johns Hopkins University Press, 1982). Made only four years after its installation, this chart may have been the first to show the Hooper Strait light vessel. An original copy is in the Chesapeake Bay Maritime Museum. Teackle's comment is in a letter of 25 February 1826 to Governor Kent, NA, Legislative Division, HR 19A, D4.1.

6. NA, Legislative Division, HR19A, G3.1.

7. LSA, Pleasonton to William Barney, 8 June 1826, 7:39.

8. LSA, Pleasonton to Barney, 30 June 1826, 7:56.

9. LSA, Pleasonton to Barney, 26 March 1827, 7:157. The statute authorizing construction of lighthouses and light vessels for several states including one at Hooper Strait was approved 18 May 1826,

Notes to Part I.

Register of Debates, 19th Congress, 1st sess., vol. II, pt 2, app., "Laws of the United States," xviii; the increased appropriation was approved 2 March 1827, *Register,* 19th Congress, 2d sess., vol. III, app., "Laws," "An Act Making Appropriations for the Support of Government for the Year 1827," v and viii.

10. Howard I. Chapelle, *The American Sailing Navy* (New York: W. W. Norton, 1949), 188, 146, and 212.

11. LSA, Pleasonton to Barney, 28 May 1827, 7:180; NA, RG 26, Deeds and Contracts, vol. E (1825-1834), 20-24.

12. LSA, Pleasonton to the President, 29 October 1827, and to Barney, 3 and 12 November 1827, 7:231-233.

13. LSA, Pleasonton to Barney, 24 November 1827, 7:245.

14. LSA, Pleasonton to Barney, 10 December 1827, 7:253.

15. Edmund M. Blunt, *The American Coast Pilot,* 12th ed. (New York: Edmund and George Blunt, 1833), 227. This was the first edition to be published after the Hooper Strait lightship entered service.

16. LSA, Pleasonton to Barney, 22 September 1828, 7:375.

17. LSA, Pleasonton to Dabney S. Carr, who had replaced Barney, 16 October 1829, 8:126.

18. LSA, Pleasonton to Frick, 10 September 1838, 13:458-60.

19. LSA, Pleasonton to Frick, 15 March and 18 May 1839, 14:230, 341.

20. *Chronicle* (Cambridge, MD), 26 February 1831 (capsized vessel); 2 July 1831 (ice damage); 31 December 1831 (off station due to ice).

21. LFS, John Hooper to Superintendent Robert Lyons, 16 October 1836 (oyster vessels).

22. *Annual Report of the Light-House Board, 1852* (Washington: GPO, 1852) 713-4.

23. LFS, Hooper to Lyons, 16 October 1836 (poor condition of vessel); LSA, Pleasonton to Robert Lyons, now Superintendent of Light Houses, Buoys, etc., for the District of Baltimore, 7 December 1836 and 9 January 1837, 11:454-5 and 481.

24. LSA, Pleasonton to William Frick, 22 November 1837, 12:430.

25. LSA, Pleasonton to Frick, 18 April 1839, 14:294.

26. LFS, Nathaniel F. Williams, Superintendent to Pleasonton, 13 March 1844,

NOTES TO PART I.

27. NA, RG 26, Records of the U.S. Coast Guard, Lighthouse Service, Annual Reports 1820-1853, box 2, entry 6, May 1845, report of Capt. Prince and F. A. Gibbons of cutter *Madison.*

28. LFS, Griffith to William H. Marriott, now Superintendent of Lights, Baltimore, 5 April 1845, and Marriott to Pleasonton, 8 April 1845,

29. NA, RG 26, Deeds and Contracts, vol. G (1839-1847), 379-382.

30. LSA, Pleasonton to Marriott, 30 August 1845 (transfer of masts, etc.), 21:145; and 30 September 1845 (new boat finished) 21:192-3; Pleasonton to Edward Green, collector, Port of Alexandria, 1 November 1845 (auction), 21:224.

31. LSA, Pleasonton to Marriott, 11 September 1845 (appointment), 21:159. Shenton and his wife Eliza are buried in the Oak Grove Methodist Church graveyard, Oak Grove, Maryland. Shenton was born 8 October 1804 and died 30 April 1873.

32. LSA, Pleasonton to Marriott, 12 February 1846, 21:367.

33. Willard Flint, *Lightships of the United States Government.* (Washington: U.S. Coast Guard Historian's Office, 1989); Records of the Lighthouse Service relating to Operation, Descriptive Lists of Lighthouse Stations 1858-1889; 1879-1939, 1858, Districts 5-11, box 1, entry 63, vol. "Light House Board, Descriptive List of Light Vessels, 5th District," 52-56.

34. LFS, Shenton to Marriot, 20 October 1845, copy to William Easby.

35. LSA, Pleasonton to William H. Cole, superintendent at Baltimore, 31 December 1847, 24:505.

36. LSA, Pleasonton to Cole, 27 June 1848, 29:435.

37. George W. Keene is buried in St. Mary Star of the Sea Catholic cemetery at Golden Hill, Maryland. His tombstone records that he died 15 December 1878 at age 80.

38. LSA, Pleasonton to Secretary of the Treasury, 4 February 1850, 29:16.

39. LSA, Pleasonton to George P. Kane, Superintendent, 21 November 1850, 29:565-6.

40. LFS, Keene to Kane, 28 December 1850.

41. NA, RG 26, entry 38, box 84, "Lighthouse Service, List of General Correspondence, 1791-1900," index cards, 24 August 1853

Notes to Part I.

and 2 December 1854 (bell); 21 February, 7 March, and 20 June 1856 (driven ashore); 22 April 1862 (cook, slave); 15 August 1862 (lantern glass).

42. NA, RG 26, United States Light House Service, "Clipping file," box 9, Hooper Straits folder.

43. "An Act Making Appropriations for Light-Houses, Light Boats, Buoys, etc.," section 2, approved 3 March 1859, cited in *Laws Relating to the Light-House Service of the United States* (Washington: GPO, 1871), 35.

44. Flint, *Lightships of the United States Government.*

45. Library of Congress: Teackle campaign speech quoted in *The Somerset Iris and Messenger of Trust,* 30 September 1828.

Notes to Part II.

II. Hooper Strait Lighthouses

1. Light-House Board, *Instructions to Light-Keepers and Masters of Light-House Vessels* (Washington: GPO, 1902, see pt. I, note 1); de Gast, *Lighthouses of the Chesapeake,* 5-6; Noble, *Lighthouses and Keepers,* 24-5.

2. de Gast, *Lighthouses of the Chesapeake,* 3-4 (quoting Mitchell's own description).

3. Annual Report, Light-House Board, 1867, 210.

4. NA, RG 26, box 168, entry 24, vols. 212 A and B. "Letters Received from District Engineers and Inspectors, February 1853-December 1900, 5th District," Letter of 31 August 1867 from Engineer A. J. Newman to Light-House Board Secretary General O. W. Poe, U.S. Army; "Marine Intelligence...Notice to Mariners," *Baltimore American and Commercial Advertiser,* 9 September 1867, 4.

5. NA, RG 26, "Letters Received from District Engineers," Newman to Poe, 18 December 1867, letter no. 160.

6. NA, RG 26, entry 16, box 8, Report of Peter C. Hains, Captain, Engineers, U.S.A. to Rear Admiral W. B. Shubrick, Chairman, Light-House Board, Washington, DC, 11 September 1871, with attached synopsis of history of Hooper Strait Light Station.

7. NA, RG 26, entry 38, box 84, index slip, 11 February 1869.

8. *Baltimore American,* 7, 12, 15, and 22 January 1877.

9. *Sun* (Baltimore), 15-18 January 1877 (description of loss of lighthouse); 24 January 1877 (Cornwell's report dated 19 January).

10. *Baltimore American,* 30 January 1877.

11. FR, Babcock to Rodgers, 19 December 1879, 380:208; 27 January 1880 (advertisement soliciting bids), 380:267; Babcock to Maltby, 2 March 1880 (accepting $150 bid for removal), 380:342.

12. David C. Holly. *Tidewater By Steamboat* (Baltimore & London: Johns Hopkins University Press, 1991), 38-9, 82.

13. Annual Report of the Light-House Board, 30 June 1878, 35; NA, RG 26, box 84, index cards for 22 January 1877, 15 March, April, and 21 November 1878, all of which refer to Hooper Strait.

14. FR, Babcock to Rodgers, 6 December 1878, 378:384.

15. FR, Babcock to Rodgers, 11 December 1878, 378:420-1; and 13 January 1879, 378:468-9.

NOTES TO PART II.

16. NA, RG 26, Lighthouse Site File, Hooper Strait, entry 66, deed dated 12 December 1878 signed by Governor Carroll.

17. FR, Babcock to A. A. McCullough, 13 January 1879, 378:473-4 and 456-8; Babcock to Shyrock & Clark, 24 January 1879, 379:13; and Babcock to McCullough, 15 July 1879, 379:366.

18. FR, Babcock to Rear Admiral John Rodgers, Chairman, Light-House Board, 7 June and 15 July 1879 (transmitting bid and contract of Poole & Hunt); and to Smith & King, 21 February 1879 (accepting bids), vol. 379. John C. Gobright. *The Monumental City or Baltimore Guidebook* (Baltimore, Gobright & Torsch, 1858), 723.

19. FR, Babcock to A. J. Hubbard, 22 August 1879, 379:450.

20. FR, Babcock to Capt. H. W. Elliott of the schooner *Vineyard*, Bishop's Head, 8 September 1879, 380:12.

21. FR, Babcock to Third District Inspector J. M. B. Olitz, 6 October 1879, 380:68.

22. FR, Babcock to Aleo, 16 and 29 September 1879, 380:24 and 53.

23. Annual Report of the Light-House Board, 30 June 1880, 35; Notice to Mariners, 30 September 1879.

24. Annual Reports of the Light-House Board, 30 June 1879, 36, and 30 June 1880 (construction, installation, and lighting).

25. NA, RG 26, entry 111, Record of Reclassification of Lighthouse Keeper Salaries, 1922-1928: Personnel Classification Board Form 14 for William O. Simpkins, sheet no. 5(b)-62, question 25.

26. Ibid., question 23.

27. United States Light-House Establishment, *Instructions to Light-Keepers* (Washington: GPO, 1881), paragraphs 34, 36, 37, 190, 191, 210, and 211.

28. Ibid., paragraph 210.

29. LHL-HS, box 200 (Hooper Strait 1879-1899), for dates mentioned in text.

30. NA, RG 26, entry 38, box 84, index card for 17 January 1891 (Harper). Harper's death was also reported in LHL-HS, box 200, 14 January 1891.

31. *Maryland & Herald,* 10 September 1918; letter of 31 May 1971 from Bozeman's daughter, Jennie Bozeman Alexander, to Chesapeake Bay Maritime Museum.

32. NA, NPRC, Hart file: Hart application of 19 March 1894;

Notes to Part II.

Gorman to Treasury Secretary J. G. Carlisle, 25 April 1894; request for and approval by Treasury of transfer to Sandy Point, 31 May and 5 June 1900; request by Light-House Board to Treasury for transfer to keeper's position at Hooper Strait, 23 December 1901; and Hart's oath of office as keeper, 28 February 1902.

33. FRL, Keeper Hart to Commander John M. Hawley, lighthouse inspector, Baltimore, 10 March 1904, vol. 176, item 262.

34. FRL, Hart to Hawley, 25 March and 6 April 1904, vol. 176; Gaskins to Hawley, 4 and 6 April 1904, vol. 177.

35. FRL, C. H. Fulcher to Commander Henry McCrae, 5th District Inspector, 6 July and 26 September 1904, 18 February and 31 March 1905; Keeper Hart to McCrae, 2 October 1904, vols. 180, 182, 186, and 187.

36. George A. Hart, Lakesville, married Fannie W. Kirwin 30 June 1897 in the Ebenezer Parsonage, Pocomoke City, Maryland. *Record of Marriages, Dorchester County, 1886-1906,* comp. B. Jean Wooston (Cambridge, MD: Weir Neck Publications, 1996), 19; Twelfth, Thirteenth, and Fourteenth Censuses (1900, 1910, 1920), Lakes District No. 5, sheets 17, 19B, and 9A. Census data show that Hart had at least seven children and that after 1900 she was known as "Mille F." Hart.

37. FRL, Hart to McCrae, 28 June 1905, vol. 190; 29 January 1906, vol. 196; 14 January 1907, vol. 206 .

38. FRL, Hart to McCrae, 22 June 1905 (report of incident), vol. 190; and 9 October 1905 (evaluation of Bradford), vol. 193.

39. LHL-HS, 1906-1933, box 201, vol. 1, 6-8 September 1908.

40. NA, NPRC, Hart file, Owens to lighthouse inspector, Baltimore, 23 October 1916.

41. NA, NPRC, Hart file, Clifford Hastings, Chief, Appointments Division, Department of Commerce, to Hart, through Commissioner of Lighthouses George Putnam, 13 December 1916. Subsequently, Acting Secretary of Commerce M. F. Sweet, in response to a letter from Fannye Hart to the President, affirmed the dismissal; Sweet to Fannye Hart, 24 January 1917.

42. LHL-HS, box 201, vol. 2, 31 December 1916 and 1 January 1917.

43. FRL, Hart to Hawley, 11 February 1904, vol. 175; Hart to Commander Edward Lloyd, Inspector, 6 February 1907, vol. 207.

Notes to Part II.

44. LHL-HS, box 201 (HS, 1906-1933), vol. 1, for dates mentioned in text.

45. LHL-HS, box 201, vol. 2 (1918); and box 202 (1936, 1940).

46. FR, Babcock to Rodgers, 22 October 1879, 380:85.

47. COR, Secretary of Commerce to Commissioner of Lighthouses, 15 July 1912, raised salaries due to addition of Honga Island; Superintendent (Baltimore) L. M. Hopkins to Commissioner, 16 August 1928 (Bentleys Point); Hopkins to Commissioner, 5 March 1930 (Crab Point).

48. COR, Inspector Ruland (Baltimore) to Commissioner, 3 May 1913 (installing either Lathrop or Rapid four-horsepower gasoline engine); Superintendent N. C. Manyon (Norfolk) to Commissioner, 30 August 1937 ("Station has recently been furnished with a new boat with a larger engine, 18-24 H.P....")

49. LHL-HS, box 202, June 1935.

50. FRL, Hart to McCrae, 13 September 1905, vol. 192, "Sir, I put the new red sectors in on the morning of the 10th." McCrae added, "Notified Board Sept. 18, 1905." Also, Light-House Board annual reports of 30 June 1882 and 30 June 1906.

51. LHL-HS, box 202, 1 November 1934: COR, L. M. Hopkins, Superintendent of Lighthouses, Baltimore, to Commissioner of Lighthouses, 15 September 1933.

52. COR, letter of 2 November 1935 from Captain Webster of *Red Star* to Superintendent of Lighthouses, Baltimore; Almy report.

53. LHL-HS, box 202, entry for 26 May 1939; COR, letter of 22 March 1939 from W. L. Rebbel, Chief Clerk, Norfolk, to Commissioner of Lighthouses.

54. *Lloyd's Register,* 1941-1942. *Itamaraty* was more than 411 feet long and owned by the Cia Nacional de Navires Corteira. She was built by Harlan & Hollingsworth, Wilmington, Delaware, in 1916, and her home port was Rio de Janeiro.

55. LHL-HS, box 202, 17 December 1941.

56. RG 26, Logs of USCG Ships and Shore Stations 1942-1947, Hooper Strait Logs, 1942-1946, box 715, USCG Logbooks-Lighthouses-Accretions, 1942, LHL-HS, 1 January 1942-30 June 1944; entries for 9 May and 27 May 1942.

57. LHL-HS, box 715: June, July, 1942.

NOTES TO PART II.

58. LHL-HS, box 715: entry for 9 December 1942.

59. LHL-HS, box 715: entry for 6 June 1944.

60. RG 26, USCG Logbooks, entry 296; LHL-HS, box 1242, 1 July 1942-27 October 1945.

61. RG 26; USCG Logbooks; LHL-HS, box 611, entry 296, 28 October 1945-11 May 1946.

62. LHL-HS, box 611: 24 November 1945 (radio watch); 4 December (running generators); 21 December (Hooper Island boat); 10 January 1946 (inspection); 12 March (shipping arms).

63. Oral history interview recorded at the lighthouse on 23 July 1987 on file at the Chesapeake Bay Maritime Museum. William Greenwood died in 1988.

64. For Hooper Strait logs from January 1948-November 1954, see RG 26, Logs of Ships and Shore Stations, boxes 1618 (30 March-15 May 1949), 1619 (16 May 1949-31 December 1950), 1697 (1 January 1951-30 June 1951), 1698 (1 January 1952-31 December 1953), and 1970 (1 January 1954-29 November 1954).

Bibliography

Blunt, Edmund M. *The American Coast Pilot.* 12th edition. New York: Edmund and George Blunt, 1833.

Chapelle, Howard I. *The History of the American Sailing Navy.* New York: Bonanza Books, n.d.; W. W. Norton, 1949.

de Gast, Robert. *The Lighthouses of the Chesapeake.* Baltimore: The Johns Hopkins U. Press, 1973.

Flint, Willard. *Lightships of the United States Government.* Washington: U.S. Coast Guard Historian's Office, 1989.

Gobright, John C. *The Monumental City or Baltimore Guidebook.* Baltimore: Gobright & Torsch, 1858.

Holland, F. Ross. *American Lighthouses, Their Illustrated History Since 1776.* Brattleboro, VT: Stephen Greene Press, 1972.

—. *Maryland Lighthouses of the Chesapeake Bay.* The Maryland Historical Trust and the Friends of St. Clements Island Museum, Inc., 1997.

Holly, David C. *Tidewater by Steamboat.* Baltimore: The Johns Hopkins U. Press, 1991.

Hornberger, Patrick and Turbyville, Linda. *Forgotten Beacons, the Lost Lighthouses of the Chesapeake Bay.* Annapolis: Eastwind Publishing, 1997.

Johnson, Robert Erwin. *Guardians of the Sea.* Annapolis: Naval Institute Press, 1987.

—. *Rear-Admiral John Rodgers, 1912-1882.* Annapolis: Naval Institute Press. 1967.

Light-House Board. *Annual Reports,* 1852-1885. Washington, DC: GPO, 1852-1885.

Lloyds of London. *Lloyds Register, 1941 1942.* London: 1942.

Noble, Dennis L. *Lighthouses & Keepers, the U.S. Lighthouse Service and Its Legacy.* Annapolis: Naval Institute Press, 1997.

Papenfuse, Edward C. and Coale, Joseph M., III. *The Hammond-Harwood House Atlas of Historical Maps of Maryland, 1608-1908.* Baltimore: The Johns Hopkins U. Press, 1982.

United States Light-House Establishment. *Instructions to Light-Keepers.* Washington: Government Printing Office, 1881.

Instructions to Light-Keepers. Photoreproduction of the 1902 edition of *Instructions to Light-Keepers and Masters of Light Vessels.* Allen Park, MI: Great Lakes Lighthouse Keepers Association, 1989.

Bibliography

United States National Archives. Record Group 26.
"Correspondence."
"Field Records of the Light-House Board and Bureau Records of the 5th District."
"Letters Received from District Engineers and Inspectors, 1853-1900, 5th District."
"Letters Sent by the 5th Auditor of the Treasury Department of the United States Regarding the Lighthouse Service."
"Lighthouse Letters Received from Lighthouse Superintendents, 1803-1852."
"Lighthouse Logs—Hooper Strait."

Witney, Dudley. *The Lighthouse.* Boston: New York Graphic Society, 1975.

Woosten, B. Jean. *Record of Marriages, Dorchester County, 1886-1906.* Cambridge, MD: Weir Neck Publications, 1996.

Newspapers

Baltimore American and Commercial Advertiser. Baltimore, 1867, 1877.
Chronicle. Cambridge, MD: 1831.
Maryland & Herald. Baltimore, 1918.
Somerset Iris and Messenger of Truth. Princess Anne, MD: 1828.
Sun. Baltimore, 1877.

Index

Acting Commissioner of Revenue, see Pleasonton, Stephen
Adams, John Quincy, 6, 49
Almy, H., 42-43
Aleo, Miguel, 29, 81
Alexandria, Virginia, 11-12
Annapolis, Maryland, 23
automation of Hooper Strait light, 49

Babcock, Orville E., 25-26, 28-29
Baltimore & Ohio Railroad, 2
Baltimore American and Commercial Advertiser, 23-24
Baltimore, Chesapeake & Atlantic Steamship Co., 34
Barbier and Fenestre, 29
Barney, William B., 4-7, 60, 64-65
Bell, Clement, 14
Bentleys Point post light, 40
Billup's Island, 24
Bishops Head, Maryland, *ix*, illustration 3, 29, 36, 45, 72
Bloodsworth Island, *ix*, illustration 3, 46, 49, 72
Blunt, Edmund, *The American Coast Pilot*, 7
Bozeman, Calvin H., 34-35, 39, 56
Bradford, Ernest L., 38, 56
Brandywine Shoals lightboat, illustration 5
Brandywine Shoals, 18
Bureau of Lighthouses, 2, 43
Burrus, O. O., 35, 56

Cambridge, Maryland, *Chronicle*, 8
Carroll, John Lee, 25, 72
Chesapeake Bay Maritime Museum, *viii-ix*, 1, illustration 15, 21, 47, 49, illustration 52-53
Chesapeake & Ohio Canal, 2
Choptank River, 15, 58
Civil War, 14
Cole, William, 13
Commerce, Department of, 2, 39, 43

INDEX

Connecticut, 15
contracts
  first lightship, 60-65
  second lightship, 66-69
Conway, Alexander S., 24, 55
Cornwell, John, 23-24, 29, 55-56
Crab Point Bar light, 40
Crapo, Maryland, illustration 3, 35
Crisfield, Maryland, *ix,* illustration 3, 23-24, 43
Croatan Light, 36
Crockett, Charles V., 15, 55

Dames Quarter, Maryland, illustration 3, 34, 40, 49
D-Day, 45
Deal Island, Maryland, 2-3, illustration 3, 48
death of U.S. President, 46
Deep Water Shoals, Virginia, 15, 59
District of Columbia, 11

Easby, William, 11, 66, 68-69
Eastern Shore Steamboat Co., 25
Eastern Bay, Maryland, 23
Easton, Maryland, 49
Eisenhower, Dwight D., 49
Experiment, U.S. Navy schooner, 5

Farrow, Clyde M., 46, 57
Fells Point, Maryland, 28
Ferguson, John, 4
fifth-order lens, 23, 29, photograph 31
Fifth Auditor, see Pleasonton, Stephen
Fishing Bay post light, 44
fog signal, *vii-viii,* 12, 23, 25, 30, illustration 32, photograph 33, 38, 40-42, 45-46, 47, 71-72
Fogs Point lighthouse, 4
Fox, Richard F., 6-7, 55
Fresnel, Augustin, 17-18
Fresnel lens, 17, photograph 31
Frick, William, 7-8
Fulcher, C. H., 36, 56

Gaskins, R. F., 35-36, 56
Gorman, Arthur Poe, 35

INDEX

Governor Robert M. McLane, police boat, 34
Great Shoals light, 45, 58
Greenwood, William: photograph 47, 47-49, 57
Griffith, Robert, 10-11, 55

Hardican, Samuel, 15, 55
Harper, Zebedee, 15, 23, 29, 34, 55-56
Hart, Fannie, 33
Hart, George A., illustration 31, 35-39, 56
Hart, Millie F., 33, 36-37 aka Fannie W. Kirwin
Hawley, John M., 35
Heliotrope, tender, 24
Holland Island Bar light, 45, 58
Holly, tender: 32, 34, illustration 34
Honga River post light, 40, 44
Hooper Island, Maryland, *ix,* 12, 13; also Hooper's Island 3, 7, 33, 72
Hooper, John, 7-10, 55
Hornet, U.S. Navy schooner, 5
Hubbard, A. J., 28-29
Hughes, J. L., Jr., 44, 57
Hydrangea, cutter, 46

Itamaraty, steamer, 43

Janes Island lighthouse, illustration 21, 25, 58
Jarrett, J. R., 35, 56
Jefferson, Joshua, 15, 55

Keene, George W., 13-14, 55
Kelly, William J., 43-44, 46, 57
Kent, Joseph, 2, 4
Kirwin, Peter, 15, 55
Kirwin, Fannie W., see Hart, Millie F.
Kohler engines, 45

Lakesville, Maryland, 36
Lathrop engine, 40
Laurel Point, North Carolina, 25
Lazaretto lighthouse depot, 26, 28
Leikam, George, 49, 57, photograph 49
Light House Service, 43, also Lighthouse Service 39
Light-House Board, 1, 15, 17-18, 20, 24-26, 29, 31-32, 34, 36

INDEX

Lyons, Robert F., 9

Madison, cutter, 11
Maltby, O. E., 24
Manyon, M. C., 44-45
Maplin Sands, Thames River, 18, illustration 19
Marriott, William H., 11, 66, 68-69
Marsh, Edna, 33
Maryland, icebreaker, 23
Maryland General Assembly, 2, 4
McCrae, Henry, 36-38
McCullough, A. A., 26
Meekins, William L., 23, 55
Messick, Harold M., 44, 57
Miles River, 50
Mister, Severn, 14, 55
Mistletoe, tender, 43
Mitchell, Alexander, 18
Murphy, Joseph, 24

Nanticoke River, *ix,* 2, illustration 3, 4, 25
Nanticoke, steamboat, 33
Nanticoke Transportation Co., 33
Narcissus, cutter, 47
Navy Point, 1
New York, 15, 29
Newton, Thomas, 4
Nonpareil, Baltimore clipper, 5

Owens, Ulman, 34-35, 39, 56
Oyster Police, 34, 39

Patapsco River, *vii,* 20
Patuxent, steamboat, 25
Pearl Harbor, 43
petitions, 2, 4, 25
Pleasonton, Stephen, 1, 4-14, photograph 9, 18, 66
Pocomoke River, 4
Poole & Hunt, 26, 28
post light, 40, photograph 41, 44
Price, William, 5, 60, 64-65
Prince, H., 11

INDEX

Pungoteague Creek, Virginia, 18, 59

radiotelephone, 43
Rapid engine, 40
red sector, 41-42
Red Star, freight boat, 42
Relief, lightship, 14
Roanoke Marshes, 36
Rodgers, John, 25, photograph 25
Roosevelt, Franklin D., death of, 46
Russell, Robert V., 38-39

Salisbury, Maryland, 25, 36, 42
Sandy Point, 35
schooner, capsized, 8
screwpile, *viii, ix,* 15, 18, illustration 19, 20-23, illustration 20, illustration 21, photograph 22, 28, 40, 50-51, 58, 70,
Sevenfoot Knoll, *ix,* 20, 58
Sharkfin light, 45, 58
Shenton, Henry, 12-13, 15, 55
Sherman, John, 29
Shubrick, William Branford, 17, photograph 17
Shyrock & Clark, 26
Simpkins, William O.: 30, 42-43, photograph 42, 57
Slocum, Washington, 15, 55
Smith Island lighthouse, 4
Smith & King, 26
Smith Point lighthouse *viii,* 59
Snow Hill, Maryland, 4
Solomons Lump light, 45, 58
Southland, freight boat, 46
St. Michaels, Maryland, 23, 50, 52
Steven's Fog Bell Apparatus, 30, illustration 32, photograph 33
Stone, Wes, photograph 31

Tangier Island, Virginia, 46
Tangier Sound, *ix,* 1, illustration 3, 4, 7, 59
Tar Bay, illustration 3, 40
Teackle, Littleton Dennis, 2, 4, 15-16
Thomas Point, *ix,* 25, 49, 58
Transportation, Department of, 2
Treasury Department, 1, 35, 66

INDEX

Tulip, tender, 24
Turley, Wm. P., 39
Tyfon air whistle, 41
Tyler, S. A., 34

United States Capitol, 28
United States Light House Establishment, 1
United States Coast Guard, 2, 37, 43, 46, 47, 48, 50

V-E Day, 46
Victor Lynn line, 42
Violet, tender, 34, 44, photograph 44
Vixen, U.S. Navy schooner, 5

Walker, Robert J., 13
Wall, Martin L., 14, 15, 55
Walter Forward, revenue cutter, 11
Wansleben, William A., 26
Webster, A. Lee, 37
Webster, see *Red Star* freight boat
Westinghouse generators, 41
Wicomico River, *ix,* 2, illustration 3, 25, 59
Windmill Point post light, 44
Wingate, Maryland, illustration 3, 36
Wisteria, cutter, 43

Picture Credits

Front cover: William C. Kepner, Chesapeake Bay Maritime Museum (CBMM). Endpapers: CBMM. 3: Eric Applegarth, CBMM. 5: Courtesy The Mariners' Museum, Newport News, VA. 9: Library of Congress. 15: William C. Kepner, CBMM. 17: Library of Congress. 19: *Report of a Tour of Inspection of European Lighthouse Establishments Made in 1873* by Major George H. Elliot, courtesy, U.S. Coast Guard Historical Office. 20: *Annual Report of the Light-House Board*, courtesy Nimitz Library, U.S. Naval Academy. 21: National Archives, Philadelphia, PA. 22: National Archives, courtesy Patrick Hornberger, Eastwind Publishing. 25: Library of Congress. 26: *Baltimore, the Monumental City*, CBMM. 27 and 28: National Archives, Philadelphia. 31: William C. Kepner, CBMM. 32: CBMM. 33: William C. Kepner, CBMM. 34: Courtesy Steamship Historical Society of America Collection, Langsdale Library, University of Baltimore. 37 and 41: National Archives, Washington, DC. 42: CBMM. 44: National Archives, Washington, DC. 47: Courtesy Mrs. William Greenwood, CBMM. 48: William C. Kepner, CBMM. 49: Courtesy William F. Leikam, Sr., CBMM. 50: Fred Thomas, CBMM. 51: Courtesy Jerry Land, CBMM. 52 Top: CBMM; bottom: courtesy Bob Roberts, CBMM. 53 Top: Fred Thomas, CBMM; bottom: courtesy M. E. Warren, CBMM.

Other publications of the Chesapeake Bay Maritime Museum:

M. V. Brewington, *Chesapeake Bay Sailing Craft*
Gilbert Byron, *Selected Poems*
Howard I. Chapelle, *Chesapeake Bay Crabbing Skiffs*
Howard I. Chapelle, *Notes on Chesapeake Bay Skipjacks*
Francis d'A. Collings, *The Discovery of the Chesapeake Bay*
Richard J. S. Dodds, *The Eastern Shore's Own Steamboat Company: The Wheeler Transportation Line of Maryland*
Richard J. S. Dodds and Pete Lesher, Editors, *A Heritage in Wood: The Chesapeake Bay Maritime Museum's Small Craft Collection*
Thomas C. Gillmer, N. A., *Chesapeake Bay Sloops*
Charles H. Kepner, *The Edna E. Lockwood*
Norman H. Plummer, *Lambert Wickes: Pirate or Patriot?*
Norman H. Plummer, *Maryland's Oyster Navy: The First Fifty Years*
From a Lighthouse Window: Recipes and Recollections from the Chesapeake Bay
John R. Valliant, *John M. Barber's Chesapeake*

These books are available from:

Chesapeake Bay Maritime Museum Store
P. O. Box 636
St. Michaels, Maryland 21663
410-745-2098
www.cbmm.org
letters@cbmm.org

Following pages:
Oil lanterns (center of top row), wick boxes, chimney lifters, and lamp feeders were among the gear supplied to lighthouse keepers by the U.S. Light-House Establishment.

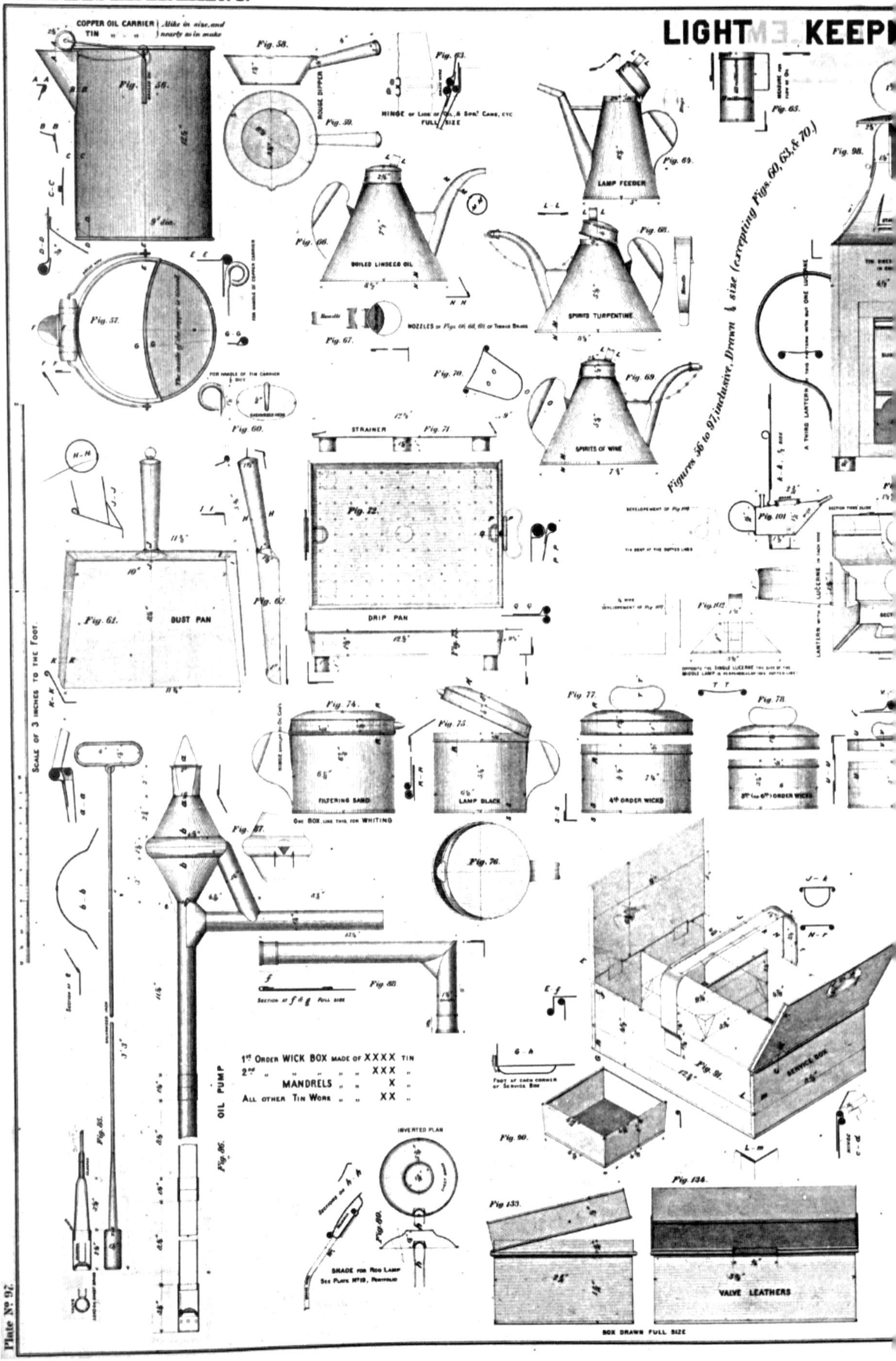
LIGHT KEEP
COPPER OIL CARRIER } Alike in size, and
TIN } nearly so in make
Fig. 56.
9" dia.
Fig. 57.
Fig. 58.
Fig. 59.
ROUGE DIPPER
HINGE OF LIDS OF OIL, & SPT. CANS, ETC FULL SIZE
Fig. 63.
Fig. 64.
LAMP FEEDER
Fig. 65.
Fig. 66.
BOILED LINSEED OIL
Fig. 67.
NOZZLES OF Figs. 66, 68, 69, OF TINNED BRASS
Fig. 68.
SPIRITS TURPENTINE
Fig. 69.
SPIRITS OF WINE
Fig. 70.
Fig. 60.
Figures 56 to 97, inclusive, Drawn ¼ size (excepting Figs. 60, 63, & 70.)
Fig. 98.
STRAINER
Fig. 71
Fig. 72.
DRIP PAN
Fig. 61.
DUST PAN
Fig. 62.
Fig. 101
Fig. 102
SCALE OF 3 INCHES TO THE FOOT.
Fig. 74.
FILTERING SAND
ONE BOX, LIKE THIS, FOR WHITING
Fig. 75.
LAMP BLACK
Fig. 77.
4th ORDER WICKS
Fig. 78.
5th (or 6th) ORDER WICKS
Fig. 87.
Fig. 76.
Fig. 80.
SECTION AT f & g FULL SIZE
1st ORDER WICK BOX MADE OF XXXX TIN
2nd „ „ „ „ „ XXX „
MANDRELS „ „ X „
ALL OTHER TIN WORK „ „ XX „
OIL PUMP
Fig. 86.
Fig. 85.
INVERTED PLAN
SHADE FOR RED LAMP
SEE PLATE No 19, PORTFOLIO
Fig. 89.
Fig. 91.
SERVICE BOX
FOOT OF EACH CORNER OF SERVICE BOX
Fig. 90.
Fig. 133.
Fig. 134.
VALVE LEATHERS
BOX DRAWN FULL SIZE

Plate No 97.